BOMBS

C000284461

An Elvington lad's war

**By
Dickie Parfitt
of
Bomber Command**

Edited by Derek Leach

Riverdale Publications 24 Riverdale River Dover Kent

DEDICATION

I have written this book for my grandchildren and great
grandchildren and hope that they will never have to face
the dangers of war. It is dedicated to the men and women
of Bomber Command – not only the aircrews but the
ground crews who kept us flying, especially the
armaments section for their courage in very
arduous and dangerous circumstances.

Copyright Derek Leach 2001
Published in 2001 by D.A. Leach (Riverdale Publications)
24 Riverdale, River, Dover, Kent CT17 0QX
ISBN 0 9536166 2 2
Printed in England by A.R. Adams & Sons (Printers) Ltd.
The Printing House, Dour Street, Dover, Kent CT16 1EW

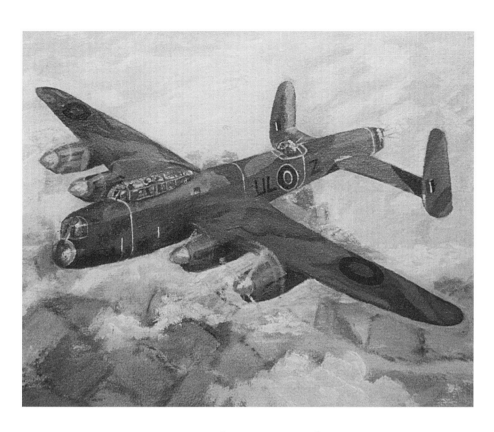

Painting of a Lancaster Bomber
by Edna Parfitt

CONTENTS

LIST OF ILLUSTRATIONS

Chapter 5

Postscript

FOREWORD

BLOWING UP THE MYTHS

Before I start my story of service in the RAF, I should explain the background so that it may be better understood.

I flew my operational raids as a bomb-aimer for Bomber Command in the last six months of the War. Some politicians and older aircrew, who flew earlier in the War, seem to think that we had it easy with all the new equipment that had been invented. But the Germans had invented things too and had upgraded their radar defences. We were attacked on daylight raids by the new jet fighters and they fired rockets into our bomber stream hoping that they would hit us. Had they homed in on us, we would have been wiped out completely in a few weeks. We were attacked not only over Germany but on our own East Coast by fighters awaiting our return. On 4 March 1945 enemy fighters shot down 27 bombers as they were coming in to land. Some of the largest aircrew losses of the War were in the last six months. In February 1945 233 aircraft and crews were lost and in March 290. More sorties, 21,191, were flown from February to March 1945 by Bomber Command and more bombs were dropped than at any other time of the War.

During the Second World War 55,573 aircrew of Bomber Command were killed and 9,784 were shot down and taken prisoner. Many more were wounded and some permanently disabled. Sir Arthur Harris, 'Bomber' Harris to the public, 'Butch' to the aircrews of Bomber Command, is one of the most controversial figures of the Second World

Air Marshal Harris, C-in-C Bomber Command
(Courtesy of Imperial War Museum ref: CH5493)

War. Even today, arguments about the bomber offensive against Germany persist. He was heavily criticised for the way he conducted 'his' war especially after D-Day and we, his aircrew, suffered because we were never given any special recognition for our efforts after D-Day despite the dangers of flying over occupied and German territory for hours at a time. A serviceman 'flying a desk' throughout the war received the same medals as we, post D-Day Bomber Command aircrew. After failing in attempts to have these efforts officially recognised, following the death of Sir Arthur in 1984, Lady Harris arranged privately for a commemorative medal to be struck for all the members of Bomber Command who served 1939-45. We had to pay £15 each for the privilege and those of us who are still alive are still bitter about this lack of recognition.

Harris took over Bomber Command in 1942 at a time when RAF losses were rising alarmingly. By July 1943 he and his crews had given Britain spectacular and much needed successes. James Hampton, author of *Selected for Aircrew* said, 'Bomber Command sustained British morale at a critical time. It sank half of all heavy German warships destroyed by the Allies; destroyed 80 U-Boats; destroyed 1,000 other ships; and delayed the use of V weapons by six critical months. When it was all over their Commander-in-Chief was denied a peerage and the men themselves were denied a campaign medal. Such treatment was unworthy.'

In September 1940 Churchill said this, 'Fighters are our salvation, but bombers alone provide the means of victory.' Despite this, Churchill became uncomfortable about the scale of destruction of German cities following the raids on Dresden in 1945 and failed to support us after the War.

According to official government historians, the bombing of German cities was a costly failure. They discovered that the government, not Harris, was mainly responsible for this policy of hitting civilian populations but also said that the War would have ended sooner if Harris had agreed to an all-out offensive against German oil installations in late 1944.

Sebastian Cox, the RAF's official historian, states that Harris took the blame for Churchill's order to support the Soviet advance by bombing eastern German cities like Dresden. Contemporary German evaluation showed that 35% fewer tanks, 31% fewer aircraft and 42% fewer lorries were made than planned. By 1944, more than a third of German industrial production was of anti-aircraft guns to attack allied bombers. In addition the Luftwaffe was unable to reinforce the eastern front because of the need to defend German airspace. Cox believed Harris's misfortune was to leave the stage to his detractors. After the War he retired to South Africa, a disillusioned man, and died in 1984. It is only now that we can show that the bombing offensive was far more effective than has previously been portrayed.

Robin Neillands, who recently produced a new book on the bomber offensive, *The Bomber War; Arthur Harris and the Allied Bombing Offensive 1939-1945*, wrote an article entitled, Blowing up the myths, in the British Legion magazine in which he shot down some of the myths. His arguments are reproduced below.

Historians allege that bombing did little to reduce Germany's military capacity and the resources devoted to RAF Bomber Command should have been diverted to the battle against the submarine or for tactical bombing in support of the Army. The allegations are not simply that the bombing offensive was a failure, but that it should never have been waged at all, that the Bomber Command aircrew of 1940-45 were terror bombers or war criminals.

Pre-War the RAF developed the bomber as a strategic weapon capable of attacking vital points in the enemy's homeland. However, when war broke out they discovered that it didn't work due to poor technology. Navigation, target-finding, bomb-aiming and the defensive capability of RAF bombers when attacked by fighters proved totally inadequate for modern war. RAF pilots had trouble finding their targets. Daylight operations were made impossible by German fighters with RAF losses in 1939-40 totalling 50% so the RAF was obliged to change to night bombing of area targets like cities, which was even more inaccurate than day bombing. A report in 1941 revealed that most bombs fell anywhere within 75 miles of the target. It took until 1942-43 to develop better navigation, target-finding and target-marking aids including the specialised marking techniques of the Pathfinder Force. In that time the Germans had developed an integrated defence of flak and fighters that largely negated the RAF improvements.

It is alleged that Sir Arthur Harris originated area bombing against German cities and civilians but it was first proposed by Air Chief Marshal Portal whilst Air Officer Commanding Bomber Command in 1940. He was an advocate of morale, or city, bombing and proposed that attacks should be made on 20 German towns after warning the citizens. Later in 1940, Portal, now Chief of the Air Staff ordered Air Marshal Pierce 'to attack the morale of the German people'. This was more than a year before Harris took over. This is no criticism of Portal. There was a war on and the choice at that time was area bombing or not bombing

Germany at all. All the technical and tactical innovations introduced by the RAF between 1939 and 1945 had the sole aim of improving navigation, target-marking and bombing in order to put the bombs on the factories and not the surrounding houses.

It is also alleged that Harris's area bombing was unnecessary because the American Air Force was able to make precision attacks on purely military targets in daylight but this is not true. Their attempts to make such attacks in 1942-43 led to horrendous losses. The German fighters found their blind spot – the front of the aircraft – and attacked from the front, closing at 600mph, with considerable nerve. The valour of the US crews deserves the highest praise. Like the British, the Americans went over to area bombing on German cities. Targets could only be hit by drenching the area with bombs. The weather over Germany for much of the year made anything else impossible. It was not until 1944 that American daylight precision bombing worked. Even then, when accuracy was good, 25,000 Berliners lost their lives during a USAAF 1,000 bomber raid on rail yards and administrative centres in the city centre in February 1945.

Harris is also accused of being callous about losses and that he didn't care about his aircrews because he rarely visited a bomber station. In fact he had to be at his HQ every day deciding how to deploy his force that night as well as fighting to get his crews the aircraft, guns, training, technical aids, pay, decorations and leave they needed. He did care about his crews and somehow they knew it – anyone who slanders 'Butch' Harris at a Bomber Command reunion is courting disaster.

The main myth concerns the 1945 Dresden raid. The popular belief that it was entirely Harris's idea is laughable. The RAF attacked Dresden once in February 1945. The Americans attacked Dresden three times after that and had attacked the city twice before the RAF. Harris had no power to order an American attack. Nor was Dresden a non-military target. Its factories included an optical works making periscopes for submarines, an electrical plant and fuses for anti-aircraft shells. The order to attack the city in February 1945 came from the Air Ministry and formed part of a series of raids on communication centres in eastern Germany. This was to support the Russian advance.

Harris's single-minded pursuit of strategic bombing did come close to obsession but like Sir Douglas Haig in the Great War, Sir Arthur Harris is being established in the public mind as an officer who was both callous and incompetent; callous with regard to his aircrews, 51% of whom were killed, and to the 600,000 German civilians killed by bombing; incompetent because his campaign achieved nothing. Incompetency was dismissed by Albert Speer, in charge of German industrial production from 1942, who said, 'the strategic bomber was the cause of all our setbacks' and the failure to stop the bombers was, 'the greatest lost battle on the German side.' The moral argument against bombing German cities is not advanced by those who suffered under Nazi rule: people in occupied territories or survivors of the concentration camps.

Harris was right to attack Germany with all means at his disposal and the surviving veterans who carried out those attacks with such determination, and at such cost, deserve our thanks and our respect.'

Max Hastings, in his excellent book *Bomber Command* said this about his research, 'As for those who flew in World War II Bomber Command, it was deeply moving to sit through a long evening in a suburban bungalow, listening to very ordinary older men describing the quite extraordinary things that they did as young men over Germany, and I am grateful that my generation has been spared the need to discover whether we could match the impossible sacrifices they made.

I also admired the bravery of the American bomber crews who knocked out, at such great loss, so many German fighters in their raids on airfields which meant that there were fewer for us to worry about!

Finally, no book about Bomber Command can overstate the contribution the Lancaster bomber aircraft made to the war effort, to quote Butch Harris, 'As a user of the Lancaster during the last three and a half years of unrelenting warfare, I would say this to the people who designed and made the plane, "Without your genius and effort we would not have prevailed. The Lancaster was the greatest single factor in winning the war".'

Chapter 1

CALL-UP

For the first two years of the War I was living at Elvington, near Dover and had watched at close hand the Battle of Britain. I had helped to catch a German fighter pilot who had landed wheels up about 100 yards from my home. I was in the Local Defence Volunteers (later renamed the Home Guard). The pilot got out of his cockpit waving his pistol but soon stopped and gave himself up when a rifle was fired at him. Two chaps took his revolver and his wallet – for which they were later fined. This was very different from what I was told to expect later when I was flying operationally.

At this same time and for nearly four years the town of Dover was constantly bombed and shelled from across the Channel. Edna, who later became my wife,

*Edna Parfitt on Dover Beach
in their courting days*

lived in Dover during the War except for a period from 1942 when she was called up to make fuel tanks for Lancaster bombers at a Frigidaire factory in London. A shell hit the house next door to her home and a few doors away people were killed. Nobody knew that shelling had started until the first shell dropped. It did not stop until Allied troops captured the gun sites. Over 2000 shells were fired on Dover.

Bearing in mind the killing, maimimg and devastation caused in Dover and all our major cities, I have little time for those in high office who blamed Butch Harris and Bomber Command for the bombing raids on German cities. For me, this was reaping the whirlwind for what was done to me and mine.

1

Call-up

I had worked in a coal mine since leaving school. During the War it was a reserved occupation and you were not called up for the armed services. When I was 21 I decided to volunteer for the forces, but the only job I could be released from mining for was as a pilot, so I volunteered for that! I received my call-up papers with a railway warrant with instructions to report to Lord's Cricket Ground, of all places, on 26 October, 1942. Looking back, I hadn't thought how Mother felt. Dad was no longer working as silicosis had taken hold and he lived on a small pension. I worked underground in a coal mine and I expect Mother felt the loss of my contribution to the family upkeep. My elder brother, Bill, became the main breadwinner with my youngest brother, Jim, just starting work. On the due date I walked to Shepherdswell Station along the old Roman Way that Roman warriors must have walked many years before me. I had been to London twice before but when I arrived it was being bombed quite severely. People were sleeping on the Underground platforms. Little did I think that in 18 months time I would be causing a great deal more trouble to the German people.

On arrival at the famous cricket ground I presented my papers to the clerk. I was now at the RAF's Aircrew Receiving Centre or 'Airsi Tarsi' as it was nicknamed. We newcomers, about 20 of us, were assembled and welcomed by the Commanding Officer, Group Captain Cunningham, who had captained Middlesex and England at cricket – hence the posting, I suppose! This was in the famous Long Room, stripped of all its trophies and pictures. I could imagine all the famous people who had entered this room and I remembered the many times I had listened on the wireless to test match broadcasts as I looked out of the windows at the pitch. Little did I know that I would meet many more famous people in the near future.

Dickie Parfitt, aged 18, just before call-up

2

Drop 'em!

Most of the group were university air squadron types, solicitors, surveyors and policemen with just two of us from coal mines, Joe Singleton and myself. I wondered what I had let myself in for, but after a few months I realised that I was quite capable of matching any of them. Next, we were lined up for the FFI (Freedom From Infection) inspection and told to drop our trousers. In walked an RAF doctor who proceeded to inspect us for VD, lice or anything else contagious. The MO (Medical Officer) proceeded down the line using his torch. Halfway down, he stopped and paid particular attention to one chap. Then he called his assistant, held a muffled conversation with him and then spoke to the chap, finally nodding and moving on. This performance took quite a time while the rest of us stood there with our trousers around our ankles! Thereafter, we had to undergo an FFI inspection on joining or leaving every station! Later, we asked the chap what had been the problem. He was reluctant to tell us but apparently he had a mole on the end of his penis and it had not reached the stage where it could be operated on, so we could expect this performance at every FFI. We told him to stand at the end of the line in future! He was known as Knobby Clark.

Next we were sent to the clothing store to be kitted out. We were given a uniform, battledress, shoes, socks etc. haversack and kit bag plus a revolver holster. I asked if we would be issued with a revolver and was told no! Apparently, under the Geneva Convention, if I were shot down and captured carrying a firearm, I could be shot as a spy. My mind went back to the ME109 pilot that I had helped capture; he carried a revolver and used it. Anyway, right through my RAF career I was never issued with a personal firearm. After kitting out we were marched to our billet which was in the wealthy part of St. John's Wood, a block of flats called, 'Abbey Lodge'. They had been taken over by the RAF and I suppose the wealthy owners had moved into the country out of the way of the bombing. With four to a room this was my introduction to community living. After settling in we were marched away for a meal
down to Regent's Park Canal, over the bridge and into the Zoo restaurant. This was to be our mess during our stay. It was half a mile from billet, so if it rained we got very wet marching there and back three times a day. There was a sergeant in charge of us – a very difficult man who didn't seem too fond of us. One Saturday night he ended up in the canal! We were all confined to barracks for three days but nobody was ever caught.

The next week was very busy. We each had three vaccinations and one inoculation – in the same arm on the same day. Afterwards we were marched to our billet and made to scrub floors. Apparently it would help the injections circulate – a likely story!

That evening I went to Edgware to see Ed. I have always called Edna, Ed. By then she had been called up to work in a munitions factory. She was on night shift but I walked to work with her and was just about ready to drop after my day. We stood outside the factory gates for a while before she clocked on and then I returned to my billet. I felt terrible and took a long time to get there. I went straight to bed but was up at 6am, marched to the Zoo for breakfast, marched back, changed into PT kit and did an hour's PT. Our PT instructor was Big John Oakes, who played football for Charlton Athletic and England before the War. During my short stay he treated me very well and always included me in the station football team which included international and first division players. Strangely enough, I played against him after the War.

My first home leave
On my first home leave I took my civilian clothes with me and went into Dover to see Ed's mother and father. I went to the pictures and the Town Hall dance. Freddie Overton was running the dances. The last bus to Elvington left at about 9.30pm so a group of us hired a taxi. The Germans were still shelling Dover and this could start without warning at any time. Entry to Dover was strictly controlled and even servicemen in uniform had to show their identity cards. At home, Dad was getting worse but Mother was holding up well. On the slow train journey back to London, stopping at every station, I thought of the carefree days before the War and 'Chippers' Cinema on Sunday nights with Eric Broadbent and Bob McCarthy. James Cagney films were always a sell out. We used to leave our bikes outside the cinema and they were never stolen.

Making music
There were several musicians in our squad and so we decided to form a group to help pass the time. We practised in our billet. I had had guitar lessons as a lad and then I had bought a new double bass from Goulden and Wind when I was about 17 and had lessons from a chap in Elvington who had been a brass band conductor in the north. I took my guitar back with me from leave but left my double bass behind!

Performing for the King
Next day back at camp, 20 of us were selected for a PT display at the Seymour Hall in front of King George VI. So the time spent with Cyril Eades doing PT

at the Barn in Elvington stood me in good stead. After the display the King walked down the line talking to each of us and asking where we came from. When I told him that I was from Dover he was very interested. 'How was the shelling?' he asked and, 'What did you do before the War?' I noticed that he had a good deal of make-up on which bothered me being just 'a little old country boy'.

After the War there was an occasion when I passed his wife, Queen Elizabeth, at close quarters. In 1965 I started a business in Dover, called Gateway Motor Factors, selling motor car spares wholesale. My suppliers invited me to the Motor Show at Earls Court on the trade day. Not having been there before, I went in what I thought was the entrance – a concrete alleyway. There was nobody about but then a tall man approached and said, 'Would you mind stepping to one side as the Queen Mother and Princess Margaret are coming.' The Queen Mother arrived, smiled at me and said, 'Good morning' followed by Princess Margaret who also smiled. They were followed by their bodyguard. It was all over in a couple of minutes. There was not a soul about. Apparently the Queen Mother had opened the exhibition and had left by the back door.

Tommy Trinder

Nearly a month went by and we were still doing drill and PT. Our little music group was getting better and we were asked to play at a concert at the Seymour Hall. The Squadronnaires Dance Orchestra was to play with Tommy Trinder as 'top of the bill'. It didn't work out like that! Trinder who was playing the Palladium could only appear as the first act. The Squadronnaires went on last and we were in the middle. The hall filled up and Trinder went out front cracking jokes, then in walked a senior officer about 5 minutes late. Trinder stood and watched him settle down, said nothing for a while and then laid into him in no uncertain manner. I don't think that officer would ever be late again for a show! The show went off all right and it was a great experience for me.

I knew that I would soon be posted so I went to see Ed as often as possible. One night I returned to the billet and found it swarming with policemen. They had arrested a chap in the next room for killing a prostitute. Later, I heard that he had been convicted and hung.

Beside the seaside

My posting came up and I was sent to the Initial Training Wing (ITW) Torquay. We were billeted in the Majestic Hotel overlooking the harbour. I noticed that over the hotel entrance was the inscription, Dom vivimus

5

Dickie's Flight at Initial Training Wing, Torquay 1943

vivamus, which was the motto of the Lafayette squadron in the First World War and meant, Whilst we live, let us live. That was quite a thought.

The CO was a First World War Canadian pilot, Squadron Leader Walker. There were better billets here with two to a room. My room-mate was a Geordie, Joe Singleton, also from a mining family. Life was much pleasanter with our own mess. Each day we marched down the hill to the main street for lessons on engines, armaments and meteorology and then back up the hill for lunch. In the afternoons we would drill or do PT and sometimes play football amongst ourselves. Our sergeant fancied himself as a footballer and was quite good. Our officer was a football and sports fanatic and entered us in the Command competition. Nearly every hotel in Torquay had a flight of trainee aircrew in it. Our officer was desperate for us to win the competition and so we did. Being in the team I could do no wrong after that.

We did have some domestic and other duties as well. One morning Joe and I were told to report to an officer in the town. Down we went complete with clean white cap flash, clean blancoed white belt, polished shoes and creased trousers. Arriving at the appointed place, we were told to report to a coal merchant in the town who told us to climb onto the back of the lorry with the sacks of coal. We then delivered to all the hotels taken over by the RAF which took all day. Joe and I walked back to our billets as black as the ace of spades! On arrival at the Majestic, our sergeant took one look at us and hit the roof. He took us to the CO who blew his top and phoned the officer concerned. He was not having his lads treated like that! We were told to clean ourselves up. Next morning the CO apologised to us and hoped that

6

we were not too upset about it. Afterwards, we both had a good laugh because we were both from mining families, well-used to being black. In fact we had enjoyed ourselves!

Our small band played at Torquay Town Hall and I was asked to do a vocal which went off quite well. I was made an LAC (Leading Aircraftman) with a small increase in pay which was welcome. Our training course was slowly coming to an end. I was called into the office and told that my aspiration to be a pilot was not to be. Apparently, with the increase in four-engined bombers, there was a need for the new position of combined bomb aimer and front gunner. With

Eric Ambler and Dickie Parfitt at Torquay

the need to improve bombing accuracy Butch Harris had decreed that this should be a specialised position.

We were interviewed individually by the CO and I was asked if I were willing to contribute weekly to the RAF Benevolent Fund. I didn't know what it was, but he told me that if anything happened to me my widow would receive a small pension. I thought for a minute and then said, 'If I was going to have my backside shot off for King and Country, I would expect King and Country to look after her!' The CO wasn't very pleased with that. However, next morning on parade, he commented that like sheep everybody had agreed to this deduction except one. On parade next day he announced that we were being posted to Manchester on the following day. He wished us luck and left. With full kit we left Torquay by rail and arrived at Heaton Park, Manchester – a large park with Nissen huts for billets. We had yet another FFI and the usual performance with Knobby Clark. Whilst there we were always on standby for Canada but we were sent to just outside Ludlow under canvas to dig a sewer!

The Parfitts' wedding photograph, 1943

Wedding bells

It was then that I arranged to marry Ed. Before I joined up I used to play double bass and guitar two or three times a week at Freddie Overton's Town Hall dances. That's where I met Ed who was a cashier at the Granada in Castle Street. After we met I always got in free to the Granada! Once we decided to marry I obtained a special licence, costing 21/6d, to marry at Ed's local church, St. Bartholomew's, at the bottom of Tower Hamlets in Dover. The site is now a block of flats. The Vicar told me that he had a son in the RAF and, if I came across him, make myself known. Fat chance, I thought, with the many thousands in the RAF and I didn't even know his name. Ed told me that his name was Basil Embrey, later Air Marshall Sir Basil Embrey! Apparently, Ed's mother had worked at the Vicarage years before the War and knew young Basil. I never met him; I wonder what sort of reception I would have got? I arranged for leave in two weeks time. I went into the office one week before to check that it was still all right and was told that I couldn't have leave because it had all been arranged in Manchester and my records were still there! However, the adjutant sorted it out and I went home as planned. My brother-in-law, who was in the RAF, was my best man and had to hitch rides home – part way on a tank – and arrived home with just a few hours to spare. Such was life in those days.

The wedding day came with our relatives present. We had our reception at the Co-op Restaurant. Ed's mother and my mother had been saving up food for months. Bob King had given some white flour to make the wedding cake; Mother had been over to Ashley for some meat; Uncle Charlie had killed a pig and Laurie Thatcher supplied the music with his accordion! Later, Laurie was one of the survivors of Arnhem. Cliff Purnell did his ventriloquist act and everyone had a good time. Last buses left at about 9pm in those days, so most people went by then. At about ten o'clock shelling began and we took to the shelters. We had arranged to stay with Ed's sister, Hilda, and that was our honeymoon. Two days after the wedding I had to report back to Ludlow. That was the last time I saw Ed for nearly two years.

Billy Liddel and guesting

Back at camp at Ludlow we were still under canvas, and still digging a sewage trench – passing time, I suppose, waiting for a boat to Canada. We returned to Heaton Park and at the first morning parade two of us were told to report to the flight commander who asked us to play football for the station against the local Marconi factory the next day. I introduced myself to the other chap and he told me that he was Billy Liddel. I hadn't a clue who he was except that he was a Scot. I played inside right and Billy was on the wing. We played well together; I laid on a goal for Billy then scored myself; then we were awarded a penalty, which, to my surprise, I was asked to take and scored; we won the match. After the match Billy told me that he was guesting for Liverpool. During the War professional footballers were allowed to play for any team convenient to them without any contracts and this was called guesting. Billy asked if I would be interested in playing for Liverpool. Back at camp, the instructors in the Physical Training Section had been talking about me apparently and I was told Billy was a Scottish international player! One of the instructors was very friendly with the Manchester United club and asked me if I would like to guest for them – would I just!

Chapter 2

CANADA

Queen Elizabeth to New York

Three days later, before anything could be arranged, I was travelling to Glasgow to catch a boat for Canada. We slept on the train seats, on the floor and in the luggage racks! Needless to say, we didn't sleep very well. On arrival we were ferried out to the ship, the Queen Elizabeth. I said cheerio to Billy and the next time I saw him was after the War playing for Derby County with two other players, Raich Carter and Peter Doherty, that I was to meet at Loughborough College in 1946. The Queen Elizabeth was an enormous ship of 80,000 tons; I hadn't been on anything bigger than a cross-Channel ferry! The Americans had taken her over, using it for trooping all over the world. She always sailed unescorted as she was so fast and no other ship could keep up with her. We were allocated cabins but slept on hammocks to fit more people in. I had never slept in a hammock before; it was fairly comfortable. I had slept in worst places! When we awoke next day, we were well on our way, north of Ireland doing 35 knots, altering course frequently. There wasn't much to do on board except sit around and watch the sea. After three days we sailed past the Statue of Liberty into New York. The next morning we went ashore with all our kit and were met by the 'Daughters of America' who gave us tea and food. Then we boarded a train for Canada. The journey to Moncton, New Brunswick, took two days and nights. We travelled through New England in the 'fall' which was a wonderful sight. We had proper sleeping bunks like you see in films, coloured attendants and meals in restaurant cars – very different to our last train journey in England!

Moncton, New Brunswick

Our stay at Moncton was short, just a few weeks, but I joined the station dance band. It was run by a sergeant who was a brass band fanatic and insisted that everybody stuck strictly to the sheet music which did little for a swinging rhythm. We did a concert in the Town Hall and a couple of broadcasts from the local radio station – most of the towns at that time had their own radio stations. Moncton was a small town and its only claim to fame was that the River Peticodiac had two tidal bores a day similar to our River Severn.

Picton, Ontario

We were then posted to Picton, Ontario. After following the St. Lawrence river through Montreal by train, we changed to a bus at Belleville for Picton. This was down a two mile causeway onto an island called Prince Edward County. We were housed in large wooden huts which were nice and warm. At breakfast somebody grabbed my arm and it was a chap from Woodnesborough who had played football with me for Deal Boys. He was an aircraft mechanic. We met quite a few times on the station and made me feel a little bit closer to home.

Our mess had what I had only seen on the movies, a juke box, which was played constantly. A favourite record was 'Oh, what a beautiful morning' sung by Frank Sinatra. I wondered who he was! Other records were also songs from 'Oklahoma' which was playing on Broadway.

Picton was No. 31 Bombing and Gunnery School. We had a few days to settle in and then started our training in earnest. First we learned to load small practice bombs and then moved on to live ones. It wasn't very pleasant, because, a few months previously, one had gone off prematurely and had injured an armourer. These 10lb bombs were for night bombing practice and smoke bombs for daylight bombing. We moved on to Browning machine guns, Morse with radio and the Aldis lamp.

No. 31 Bombing and Gunnery School, Picton

The time came for my first flight. I was issued with winter kit: fur boots, zip up trousers, fur coats, flying helmet, goggles and fur gloves. I went up on 20 November 1943 in an Anson piloted by a Sgt. Morton. It was a 'wind strength and direction finding' flight. This was essential for all types of bombing using bomb sight Mark 9 and 14. Ansons were easy to fly with canvas-covered bodies and undercarriages that you wound up by hand; it was easy winding them down but winding them up was hard, especially wearing full winter flying kit. It would soon make you sweat and this wasn't good when the temperature was nearly 40 degrees below!

A small group of us palled up. Among them was Doug Hillier from the West Country, a Free Frenchman whom later we had to leave behind in Canada at a VD hospital and Chiefy Reed, a flight sergeant ex fighter pilot. I never did find out anything about him but it was rumoured that he had pranged a Spitfire by flying down the wrong runway. Doug and I went on many leaves to America – Watertown, Buffalo and Rochester in New York State.

Winter set in and it was very cold. I tried ice skating but wasn't very good at it. We challenged the instructors to a game of ice hockey. This was not a good idea as most of them were Canadians. I was put in goal and was offered all the kit: knee pads, shoulder pads, gloves and helmet. 'Do I need all this,' I said. 'Wait and see,' I was told. I had not realised how hard the puck was! Needless to say, we were overwhelmed. I played basketball for the station team. All these activities were arranged through the Salvation Army by a chap named Mac. Strangely enough, home in Dover many months later, Ed and I met him at the bottom of Tower Hamlets. He was with the Canadian Army stationed at the Castle barracks.

The next flight was in a Bolingbroke, a Canadian-built Blenheim. Two of us collected our belts of .303 bullets, the heads of which were painted, one red and one blue, so that when they went through the canvas drogue they would leave a coloured mark identifying our strikes. Off we went. I was first into the gun turret; it was a tight fit and I had to load my two belts of bullets into the guns which was very difficult in the cramped conditions. I called the pilot on the intercom when I was ready and he, in turn, called up the pilot of the Lysander towing the drogue. When the drogue came within range I got it in my sights, pressed the trigger and the twin guns belched out. The drogue went flying off the end of the cable and the Lysander lunged forward; it must have frightened the life out of the Lysander crew. My pilot saw what had happened and called the exercise off. Both planes returned to base and we found that I had shot the cable through. The pilot wasn't pleased because we had to do it all over again. The Bristol gun turret had a see-saw motion and when you fired towards the tail there was an automatic cut-out to prevent you hitting the tail but, a week earlier, the cut-out had failed to operate and the bullets had cut half the tail fin off; the pilot was not amused but managed to fly back to base and land safely.

Watertown, New York State

Training continued with some 48 hour leave passes when Doug and I set out for America hitch-hiking to the 1000-island bridge into New York State and eventually arriving at Watertown. F.W. Woolworth had opened his first shop there which had grown into a large complex. We stayed in a hotel in the centre of town and set off next day to look around. The huge army camp had emptied of soldiers, presumably off to Europe and the Second Front, so we had the town to ourselves. We went to the USO (the American equivalent of the NAAFI) and were told that there was a list of people who would invite us to stay with them, many from the 'old country'. We were allocated to someone who owned a funeral parlour which we didn't know anything about. We slept above the room where the bodies lay and were a bit apprehensive. Later, we were shown around the business. I had never seen anything like it – high powered. We only stayed the one night and back at the USO we were given another address, a single man, named Lucius Carpenter, whom we stayed with twice more. It wasn't until our second visit that we discovered he was gay. At that time I had little knowledge of homosexuals. He treated us very well. Doug had a posh accent and looked like Arthur Treacher, a film star who always took the part of an English butler; the Americans loved that. In one bar we visited, the barman wouldn't serve me as he thought I was under age. After a while, a plain clothes policeman asked who we were and when we told him, he treated us to a drink and left. I wrote to Lucius after the War, but received a reply from a relative saying that Lucius had died.

Back at Picton training continued. It was now full winter and very cold. I was due to go skeet (clay pigeon) shooting. I didn't feel very well, but I went. After a while in the open air I felt very ill and cold and was rushed to hospital. It was only flu and after a few days I was a bit better and was sent to a local farming family to recuperate. Returning to training, the instructors pushed me hard as I was a week behind.

We went to Watertown once more and stayed with Lucius. Coming back we arrived at the ferry, hoping to be rowed across instead of going right round the lake some 40 miles or so. The lake had frozen over, but the ferryman suggested that he accompany us across the ice on foot! He assured us that it was quite safe with ice at least four feet thick and he had marked out a path. We set off. I don't know what was worse: my first shift down the mines, my first bombing operation over Germany or this. Anyhow, we made it and were directed to a large fish hatchery where we could phone for a taxi. Whilst waiting, we were shown around the hatchery where there were millions of small fish. After a coffee – not much tea is drunk over there, of course – the taxi arrived to take us back to camp. Who said that I couldn't walk on water?

Niagara Falls

I was now doing practice bombing by night and lessons by day. After another few weeks we had another 48 hour pass. This time we set off for Toronto. We were hitchhiking again and had several lifts, mainly from people whose parents were from the 'old country' and we had several invitations to their homes. We were picked up by a young lady who told us she had been to a physical training college in England at a place called Nonington. When I told her that I lived about two miles from there, she was amazed and asked us to meet her family. As it was our last chance to see Niagara Falls we had to decline. Once we got through Toronto onto the Queen Elizabeth Highway, a three lane motorway in 1943, we were soon in Niagara. Next day, we crossed over the Falls on the Rainbow Bridge and saw the small boat that sails right up to the Falls. The noise of the water was terrific. On arrival at the American side of the Falls, the Customs men took a lot of convincing as to who we were; however, we convinced them and went into Buffalo and stayed one night before returning to Picton.

In a few weeks time we would be taking our final exams. The exam weeks started and halfway through I received a telegram telling me that Dad had passed away. The instructor was very understanding but I told Doug that I had expected it after seeing Dad before I left England. I wrote to Mum and continued with my exams. Seven days leave followed when Doug and I went to Watertown again and on to Rochester. We went on to Buffalo, through Canada to Toronto and back to Picton. A few days later we were posted to No. 1 Central Navigation School, Rivers, Manitoba. So we said farewell to the staff and Salvation Army Mac.

Rivers, Manitoba

We enjoyed another long luxurious train journey of two days around the picturesque Lake Erie. From Winnipeg we had a two hour drive in a bus. Rivers had a grain elevator and about a dozen houses. My first flight here was a familiarisation flight in a Faithful Annie (Anson). Unusually, it was started up in the hangar, the doors opened, we taxied out and the doors were immediately closed behind us. It was that cold. I sat in the co-pilot's seat. After winding up the undercarriage with some difficulty, the pilot told me to sit at the navigator's table, he would fly around, point to an area on the map and I had to tell him where we were. I didn't have a clue! He then pointed to a town on the map and then to what I would call a village on the ground. 'That's a town?' I said and he nodded. It was the grain elevator with the twenty houses.

We had been flying for about an hour and I went back to the navigator's table to give the pilot a course for the bombing range. In the process of finishing my notes, I saw out of the corner of my eye somebody pass through to the back of the aircraft. I looked up and saw that it was the pilot using the Elsan toilet. The pilot's seat was empty. The pilot came back, looked at me and laughed. We were flying on 'George', the automatic pilot!

During my stay at Rivers I played with the station dance band. Another trainee played the piano, Wally Mesher, a policeman from Scotland Yard. In 1948 I saw him getting off a train at Folkestone but he was gone before I could catch him.

In the hangar one day getting ready for a flight, a Dakota of the American Air Force taxied in, bad weather had forced it down. On board was a group of actors and actresses doing their rounds entertaining American troops – we were close to the U.S. border. As they came off I spoke to some of them one of whom I recognised as Kathryn Grayson, the film star, but she looked very ordinary!

Passing Out class, Rivers, Manitoba

During my six week stay at Rivers I did map reading, navigation, pin pointing and photography. At the end we were presented with our wings and promoted to sergeant or pilot officer. We were given rail tickets to St. Johns, New Brunswick with 21 days to get there. Doug and I decided to go to Denver, Colorado. We had been invited down there by an aunt of one of the chaps. We intended to fly from Winnipeg Airport but there were no flights to Denver. So we went to the railway station. As we entered the main hall we noticed that there were several tramps on the seats, most were drunk on hooch (wood alcohol) as you could only drink in hotels or in your own home; there were no pubs as such. They were looking for handouts but a Mountie appeared and cleared them out in no uncertain fashion. Wood alcohol was known to make people blind. We were forbidden to drink it. We were also forbidden to give or supply alcohol to the Red Indian population. You could buy a liquor licence for a dollar which enabled you to buy at the local liquor store but it could only be consumed in your home or hotel room.

We decided to forget about Denver and make for Detroit. First we took the train for a few days to Toronto, hitch-hiked down the Highway on our way to London, Ontario. Most of the inhabitants in this area were of English descent and we were never short of lifts. We crossed the border to Detroit and found the USO who fixed us up with a stay at a private house. When we went out next day there were race riots going on, blacks were chasing whites and vice versa. Apparently the Mayor had given the blacks some concessions in return for their votes and this didn't go down very well with the whites. We quickly moved on toward St. Johns. There were still plenty of lifts and we were always asked what we were. To prevent misunderstandings we told them we were 'bombardiers' in the British Air Force. This conjured up all sorts of things in their imaginations: that we had already flown a lot of bombing raids and were young heroes. The more we denied it, the worse it got.

Dorsey and Sinatra

Our next stop was Cleveland, Ohio. The USO gave us a place to stay again plus tickets for a show. It was Tommy Dorsey and his band with a singer I didn't know too much about, Frank Sinatra. We were given a lot of attention at the show with special seats. I enjoyed it tremendously as Dorsey was the greatest in my estimation. First, Dorsey played a couple of his standards then Sinatra came on and the audience, mainly girls, went berserk, screaming like mad. I couldn't believe it. It was deafening and this happened every time he sang. At the end we were asked if we would like to meet Tommy Dorsey, so we went round to the stage door and were introduced to him, his band and this chap Sinatra – a weedy looking bloke about the same age as myself. As we came out, the girls were crowding the stage door. Now, looking back on Frank Sinatra's long singing career, I much prefer his timing and phrasing in his later years.

We had plenty of invitations and the next night we were invited to a night club where we were wined and dined. There was a band and Doug mentioned that I was a singer in a dance band, so I was promptly asked to sing. I could have murdered him! Anyhow, I sang 'The White Cliffs of Dover' and 'We'll meet again' which had them crying. I was asked to sing again the following night but we needed to move on as our time was running out. We called at Niagara Falls and Buffalo again and went on to Rochester and looked around the town, the home of Kodak cameras. We went on to Watertown where Lucius had a meal waiting for us. We talked well into the night but were up early, said farewell to a tearful Lucius and made our way back to Canada. At Montreal we managed to get places on the train for St. Johns when we told them it was essential for us to get back in time for the boat to England. We were given a sleeper which was just as well because the journey took two nights and a day.

Red lights and redcaps

Arriving at St. Johns in the morning we had a look round this big seaport. At midday we decided to have a meal and went into a reasonable looking restaurant run by Chinese. After a few minutes a couple of RCAF policemen came in and asked us what we were doing, 'Having a meal before embarking,' we said. 'OK, have your meal and get out smartly,' came the reply. I asked what was the problem and was told that the place was out of bounds. It was a brothel! However, they let us finish our meal and then took us to our boat.

The Louis Pasteur, a French ship, was not as big as the Queen Elizabeth but it had won the Blue Riband on the South American route and so we sailed unescorted, except for brief visits by Catalina and Sunderland flying boats, back to Liverpool. During the voyage we had to take turns mounting the machine guns on the top deck now that we were trained as gunners. The ship moved very fast at about 35 knots, changing course every few minutes.

Chapter 3

TRAINING IN ENGLAND

Leslie Ames

From Liverpool we went to Harrogate, billeted in the Grand Hotel. Being sergeants now, the rooms were quite good and we got a good night's sleep – the first for some time. With a 48 hour pass I went back to Dover. Ed had finished at the munitions factory in London and had set up home above a butcher's shop in Tower Hamlets. She had also managed to get some furniture coupons. This was our first home together. Ed was working for the Prudential collecting the tuppence a week insurance premiums that people paid in those days.

Back in Harrogate, I was sent for by the CO who was none other than Leslie Ames, the Kent and England batsman and wicket-keeper, who was now a squadron leader. He had noticed that I was from Dover. I knew that he was from Elham and had played football for Folkestone. He asked me to sit down, much to the annoyance of the adjutant, and we talked about Harry Warren, Charlie Godden and Folkestone. Then he told me that I was being posted to Whitley Bay and wished me well.

Whitley Bay

We were billeted in terraced houses, just off the seafront and were told that this was a sort of commando course with plenty of PT and early mornings. One day we were driven out into the country and told to find our way back, living off the land and relying on maps. All the signposts in the country had been removed to confuse the enemy if they invaded. I managed all right as I had spent a great deal of my youth playing in Toy Woods at home. We slept in a barn. The farmer was suspicious thinking that we were spies particularly as we were wearing working battledress with no badges or rank insignia. We did convince him and he offered to take us back in his tractor and trailer, but we refused. We did two more of these exercises which were meant to help us if we were shot down and had to find our way home. We finished the course and were posted to Northern Ireland. Join Bomber Command and see the World! It was a very rough crossing from Stranraer to Larne and, although I was a good sailor, when I saw the sailors being sick I joined them! That was a day to remember because when we landed at Larne we were told it was D-Day – the Allies had landed in France.

Northern Ireland

We were billeted at Bishopcourt, south of Belfast, in Nissen huts that were always quite damp but life was not too bad – as sergeants we had somebody to clear up after us. We started flying in later versions of Ansons with hydraulic undercarriages – no more winding up and down, thank God. There was a lot of practice bombing with 10lb flash and smoke bombs and navigation trips around the west coast of Scotland and the Irish Channel. On one longish trip, the pilot was worried about running out of fuel and we put down on the Isle of Man to refuel and got back safely. One of the ground staff, a Scot, played the bagpipes, so we had to march behind him on church parade. He wasn't very popular. In the few weeks at Bishopcourt we had a couple of leave passes and went to Belfast, where we were treated very well, but the locals didn't like us very much.

Hixon, Staffordshire

It was now August, 1944. Time moved on and so did we – to Hixon in Staffordshire where we were to be crewed up on Wellingtons. Here I lost contact with my good friend, Doug Hillier. I was introduced to my crew: Flight Sergeant (Taffy) Burnel, the pilot, Sergeant Ron Watson, navigator, Flight Sergeant William (Pat) Mumford, wireless operator from Australia, Sergeant Mickey Lobzinger, mid/upper gunner from Canada and Sergeant Sid Witt, rear gunner from Canada. As we had no flight engineer I was acting as flight engineer and second pilot as well as being the bomb aimer! For the first few days we did 'circuits and bumps' in the Wellingtons. I was also doing some time each day in the pilot trainer aircraft with Taffy giving me some tips, so that in an emergency I could fly a plane.

Crews took turns using the Wellingtons. When we were doing landing practice, waiting our turn, we watched other crews performing. At one end of the runway was the main railway line and it was important to keep that in mind when landing. One plane landed too far down the runway, overshot and ended up on the railway line breaking its back. We and the 'blood wagon' rushed over to see two white-faced Air Training Corps lads looking out of the front half, staring into space but luckily unhurt. No more ATC lads were allowed to fly after that.

We did cross country flights and bombing using radar. On one of these flights we had problems with the radio and started back to base. The weather was bad and closing in, we were navigating on dead reckoning without the use of radio or radar. Over our base we had to try and break cloud. Taffy asked me to go to the front to look for a position. Suddenly we broke cloud and I saw that we were among some tall chimneys! 'For Christ's sake, get up,' I shouted to Taffy which he did. Fuel was low and we were on the reserve. Fortunately, Pat had repaired the radio and called for assistance. Ground control gave us directions telling us that cloud was less than 500 feet above the runway. Taffy decided that it was 'shit or bust' and in we went. I was still at the front. We broke cloud at 400 feet, did a circuit and landed. We all went out for a drink that evening!

Back home

The course finished and we were given seven days leave. Pat, Sid and Mickey took their chance to see London whilst the rest of us went home. In Dover the German cross-Channel guns were still active. I went to our new flat. There was no way of letting Ed know when I would arrive but fortunately she was there. It was the end of November, 1944 and the weather was cold. We visited my Mother on the Saturday who had the usual big coal fire and a good tea. In the evening we went to our local pub in Dover with Ed's father, an ex-Marine who was always proud to go with us. Then it was back to our flat to listen to Saturday night 'Music Hall' on the wireless. During the next few days we scoured the second hand shops for furniture which was 'off coupons'. We went to the pictures, to the Plaza. We had to queue to get in but the manager recognised Ed – she had been the cashier at the Granada and knew him quite well – took us in and gave us free seats. Two days later, he was found murdered in his office. A local lad of 18 was arrested and convicted. Time flew by and I left for my new posting, the Heavy Conversion Unit (HCU) at Lindholme near Doncaster.

Lindholme

First I met the new member of our crew, Reg Grout, our flight engineer. He seemed very young, straight off his course with not a lot of flying experience. Taffy had been promoted to Pilot Officer. We should have flown the next morning but Sid had not arrived. Taffy was very upset about it. When Sid arrived the next day the CO had him in and gave him a good ticking off. Later, I asked him why he was late back. Apparently, he had picked up this girl and stayed with her and was very reluctant to leave her. Knowing Sid, I could well believe it!

We were now flying Halifax aircraft doing the usual navigation and bombing flights. I was now using the Mark 14 semi-computerised bombing sight and the H2S radar equipment which was used when over cloud. On a navigation training flight we were second to take off. The plane in front took off down the runway, lifted off the ground, then suddenly took a nose dive and went up in flames. By this time we were on the way down the runway preparing for lift off. It was too late to stop, so Taffy slammed the throttle through the 'gate' and took off, did a circuit and landed. Some of the crew of the burning aircraft got out, others were killed. They had just joined the station and I didn't know them very well.

Within the next few days we moved on to Lancasters and did a week's conversion course, mainly for the pilot's sake. It was a good plane to fly in. At long last we were ready for an operational posting. Now that we were all at least sergeants, we didn't have to have an FFI on leaving the station!

Chapter 4

OPERATIONAL

Fiskerton

We arrived at Fiskerton, just outside Lincoln. It was a fairly new aerodrome and one of the few to have FIDO (Fog Investigation Dispersal Operation) which was a series of pipes running down each side of the main runway into which fuel was pumped and then lit. The flames dispersed any fog. It was like landing in a huge tunnel and if you had any problems with the landing gear, like a burst tyre, and swivelled into the flames, you just went up in flames too! Nevertheless, with fog frequent in the flat country of Lincoln, we thought it was a good idea, but soon thought otherwise because we were still flying when every other aerodrome was fog bound and it was dangerous to land in. FIDO was introduced in November 1943 and 2,486 aircraft landed with its aid at 15 airfields at a cost of 100,000 gallons of fuel.

We settled into our hut where we had one airman to look after the billets, keep the place clean, light the stove and make sure we had hot water on our return from an operation, no matter what time of the day or night. As we were about a mile from the base we were issued with bicycles.

Lancaster taking off using FIDO (courtesy of Imperial War Museum ref: CH15272)

A bomber crew

In a bomber aircrew the pilot was the crew captain, whether an NCO or not he was superior to any officer in the crew. He made the decisions, although, if sensible and there was time, he would consult the crew first. Officer pilots of crews that completed 30 operations usually received the Distinguished Flying Cross on behalf of their crew, but NCO pilots would receive the Distinguished Flying Medal which were seldom given.

The navigator was the hardest worker in the crew – pilot included. A flight could last from four to nine hours and he would be working all the time. The pilot could take a rest because most of the time the aircraft would be on 'George', the automatic pilot. Timing was the navigator's responsibility, but even at best he was only as good as his pilot flying the correct course, height and speed advised by the navigator. This was duly noted in his log and woe betide any pilot who did not conform because the navigator's log was always checked at debriefing after an operation. I saw pilots demolished by the squadron navigation officer with threats of demotion. It was a very skilled trade carried out under trying, cramped conditions with an oxygen mask on most of the time which did not help concentration. Navigating involved measuring angles and distances on the Mercator Projection Chart in poor light, taking a radar fix every six minutes, fixing wind speed and direction and estimating time of arrival. Winds could change very quickly and could be 100 mph at 20,000 feet.

Navigator at battle stations
(courtesy of Imperial War Museum ref: CH12288)

Dropping bombs in the right place especially at night required precision and courage. It was no use flying all the way to the target, putting every member of the crew at risk, and then missing the target. This was the bomb aimer's job. He alone would be looking straight down at the flak. It was an awesome sight to see the flak coming straight at you and bursting all around; to see a Lancaster, silhouetted against the burning target, being hit and blown up right in front of you; to see one of our own bombers dropping a stick of bombs onto another Lancaster; or to watch the searchlights groping around ever closer, knowing what was in store for you if they caught you in their beams. Throughout an attack, he would calmly give instructions to the pilot and keep his nerve until the target was in his bombsight. Then he would go through the bombing sequence with only quarter inch perspex shielding him from the flak. When flying a four-engined bomber with Rolls Royce Merlin engines going flat out, wearing a flying helmet with intercom headphones on, we could feel but not hear the explosions of the anti-aircraft fire directed at us – except when either you or the plane were hit which I can verify from my own experience! At 79 years of age I still suffer from noises in the ears – known as 'Lancaster ear'. I am full of admiration for those who could hear the explosions all around them – soldiers going up the beaches on D-Day and in other fields of war, sailors in naval battles etc. Equally frightening must have been the silence of jungle warfare, not knowing when you would be fired on.

When the order 'Bomb doors open' was given by the bomb aimer, the pilot

Bomb aimer at battle stations (courtesy of Imperial War Museum ref: CH12283)

had to repeat it. The noise of the wind rushing through the bombs in the bomb bay was eerie. The rest of the crew had their intercoms switched on but had to maintain silence except in an emergency – whilst giving instructions the bomb aimer could hear the heavy breathing of the rest of the crew over the intercom. The chief crime of the bomb aimer was to undershoot the target. This is where the Master Bomber and his backers-up took control of the raid and guided the bomb-aimers with the use of marker flares. Once the bombs were dropped, the bomb aimer called, 'Bombs gone' (not 'Bombs away' which the Americans used), the bomb doors remained open so that the aircraft flew level to enable accurate photographs to be taken. The heavy breathing silence continued until the bomb aimer called, 'Bomb doors close' to the pilot and everybody heaved a sigh of relief.

The flight engineer's job was to monitor the instruments constantly, in particular checking fuel consumption and to help the pilot generally. He also helped the bomb aimer by 'windowing' which was to throw out metallised strips of paper to confuse enemy radar. He kept a log of all his activities which would be checked at debriefing with the squadron engineering officer. Woe betide any pilot who flogged his engines. They were the pride and joy of the Engineering Officer and would be needed on the next operation. He had usually done at least 30 operations himself and knew a lot about engines.

The wireless operator, or WOP as he was known, was responsible for operating the radio, the radar jamming devices and worked 'fishpond' which was radar that picked up other aircraft close by. He gave the gunners warnings of fighters about.

The two gunners had lonely jobs and could not relax. The lives of the rest of the crew rested upon their vigilance. The tail gunner never saw another member of his crew throughout the flight. They discouraged any attack and were rarely given second chances by attacking fighters.

It is a fact that some crews, both RAF and American decided, to fly to Sweden and Switzerland, neutral countries, and were detained for the rest of the War. The reasons for this are debatable but they were out of the War! In the early stages of the War, some aircrews at the first sign of flak simply dropped their bombs anywhere and turned for home. Two ex-Navy friends of mine were sunk and made prisoners of war and then were forced to work in the Hamburg shipyards. When the sirens sounded they were told to keep working such was the inaccuracy of our bombing early in the War with only 4 to 6% falling on or near the target. This is what Sir Arthur Harris, or 'Butch' Harris as we called him, had to remedy when he took over Bomber Command in late 1942. He immediately installed line overlap cameras on aircraft to photograph where the bombs were dropped. When the bomb aimer pressed the bomb tit and the first bombs were released, the camera started and a photo flare was released exploding over the target enabling photographs to be taken by day or night. This made the bomb aimer accountable for where the bombs were dropped. Butch Harris made us aware of the need for teamwork; everyone had their important part to play in a successful operation.

Where's the MO?

We all went into Lincoln that night for a drink and a look round. You must remember that we were all very young, 19½ to 24 years old. Next morning we cycled down to the Sergeants' Mess for a 'flying breakfast' of fried egg, bacon and fried bread and then reported to the Squadron Commander, Squadron Leader Blemier-Hasset. He welcomed us to 576 Squadron, told us what to expect and not what to do. Then he said, ' Before you go, I need to tell you that we have a Medical Officer here and as you are a sprog (new) crew, he will come to you just before take off, complete with flying gear and will ask you to take him with you. He will tell you that he is experimenting with the use of oxygen for aircrew. You are not to take him with you and you will be in deep trouble if you do!' Later that evening I found out what this was all about. Apparently, the MO had been on more operations, unofficially, than most aircrew! This had been going on for some time until one day there was a panic on the station and the MO was nowhere to be found. He was over Germany on a raid. Consequently, he was banned from flying. His name was Nigel Henderson. Later, I met up with him again at No. 1 Medical Rehabilitation Unit at Chessington and, knowing him there, I could well imagine the things he got up to on the squadron.

We each went to our appropriate sections; I went to the Bombing Section and was welcomed by the Bombing Leader. Another bomb aimer showed me around a Lancaster in the hangar and explained the modifications I needed to know about including how to release manually the 4,000lb 'cookie'. There is a story attached to this. Whenever an aircraft went into a hangar to be worked on, all bombs were taken off before it went in; however, on one occasion a 4,000lb blockbuster bomb was left in the aircraft and nobody knew. A new bomb aimer, like me, was being shown around and then the instructor said that he would show the bomb aimer how to release the cookie manually if it got stuck in the bomb bay over the target. He grabbed the lever and pulled; there was a dull thud as the bomb landed on the closed bomb doors. Both of them turned pale realising what had happened. Ground crew grabbed a lifting trolley and pushed it underneath because the bomb's weight was forcing the bomb doors open. That stopped it. Everybody breathed a sigh of relief; however, it would not have gone off as the fuses were safe! Just one of the things that could happen before you even got off the ground!

Seniority rules, OK

Also in the hangar was the aircraft allocated to us, ULZ. Being the junior crew we got the oldest aircraft which had done a great number of operations, hopefully a good omen for us. The senior crew always got a new aircraft straight from the factory and the other aircraft were then passed down the seniority line! This rotation also occurred when a crew completed 30 operations and left the squadron for a well-earned rest; also, when an aircraft was shot down and did not return, then a new aircraft was allocated to the squadron. So, your crew was constantly moving up the ladder until it became the senior crew.

Seniority also applied to take off and landing on return, always the senior crew first with no queue jumping unless there was an emergency. Spacing and timing of take off was critical especially when taking part in 1,000 bomber raids. This was worked out by HQ but there were always some clowns, who were dealt with severely. Around Lincoln there were at least seven aerodromes with their circuits crossing one another with the inevitable collisions.

Escape kit

Next, we had our photographs taken as a crew in front of a Lancaster, plus three individual passport photographs, because if we were shot down we would need a passport photograph for the French Resistance to make a false passport to help

 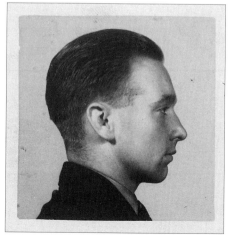

'Passport' photos of Dickie Parfitt

us get home; they were very short of photographic material. We were issued with various escape gadgets: a small compass, a button compass and I had a three inch piece of hacksaw blade sewn into my battledress collar! There was also a first-aid kit with a syringe of morphine and, on most flights, 1,000 francs which had to be signed for and taken back on return. This was to bribe the French to help us if shot down.

That evening we all went to the mess for our evening meal minus Taffy, our pilot, who had gone on his first operation with the flight commander to be blooded. He got back safely and joined us later.

Next day we had a session in the decompression chamber with each of us taking turns to take our oxygen masks off, simulating flying at 25,000 feet. It was a strange feeling; for the first minute it was all right but then you gradually lost your senses and, if you went too long, you could suffer brain damage. This was important for me because I would be the only crew member changing positions on the aircraft. I became very concerned about the small oxygen bottles on the aircraft which enabled me to move about and always checked mine religiously but the others didn't. Hence the problem I had later with Pat, our wireless operator, when I had to get him out of trouble during an operation.

A lecture on how to escape followed. If we had to bale out over enemy territory, we were advised to take a 'wakey, wakey' tablet first to compose ourselves! I used them on most of my night raids to help keep me alert and awake. We were shown how to use the morphine syringe if injured and told to try and contact a friendly group!

My first op

On the notice board as we went in for our midday meal the daily 'Battle Order' was up and we were on it. The time had come 'to face the dreaded Hun' – the favourite phrase of my good friend Herbie Goodborn. What is more, I would be sitting on a bomb load for the first time!

After our meal we went to our aircraft and asked the ground crew the size of the fuel load. It was 1200 gallons which was about enough for the Ruhr and back. That turned out to be it. Our bomb load was a 4,000lb blockbuster, or cookie as it was commonly known, plus 16,000lbs of incendiary bombs. I went to the front of the aircraft and loaded my two Browning .303 machine guns in the front turret, checked them ready for use and put the safety catch on. Then I checked my small oxygen bottles, the bomb sight and computer and made sure all my switches were off. I also checked the packages of 'window' (metallised strips of paper) to drop prior to the run over the target in order to try and jam the German radar defences. At the navigator's table I checked the radar with

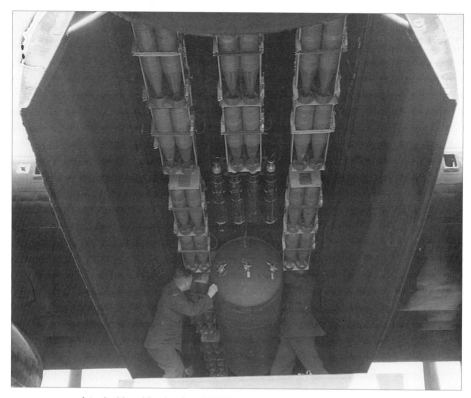

A typical bombing load: a 4,000lb cookie surrounded by incendiaries
(courtesy of Imperial War Museum ref: CH17458)

Ron, our navigator and checked the master compass in the fuselage – this was most important for the radar equipment and my bombsight.

I left Ron in the aircraft and climbed down to the deck and saw for the first time the 4,000lb cookie on the trolley, all fused-up with the incendiaries behind. The flight sergeant armourer saw me and came over. 'Is this your first,' he said. I nodded. 'Right, stick with me and we'll go through it together.' The rest of the crew had completed their checks and gone off, so here I was, 23 years old, surrounded by 20,000lbs of bombs, 1200 gallons of fuel and 30,000 rounds of ammunition! I fancy the rest of the crew didn't fancy all that TNT – neither did I. I had joined up to be a pilot, not a bomb aimer!

My preparation for the operation began. Then I reported to the Bombing Leader who had some advice and some warnings to give, mainly about 'creeping back' during the raid. This was the tendency during a raid, which might last an hour, for bombs to go off target gradually unless corrected by the Master Bomber. I went on to the Map Section and collected the necessary bumph, then headed for the briefing room. There was a huge map of Western Europe on the wall with tapes to indicate our tracks and turning points to the target which was Duisberg in the Ruhr. We had guessed correctly from the fuel load. I joined Ron at his table who was already busy drawing courses on his map. Later we were joined by the rest of the crew. When they saw the target you could feel the sense of anticipation, fear and tension despite the jokes and remarks. Sid, our rear gunner had a dry sense of humour and could always raise a laugh, but on the actual trips he would say very little; rear gunner was a very lonely job.

The briefing

The briefing was opened at 1430 by the Squadron Commander followed by the Intelligence and Met. Officers and Section Leaders. Only the pilot, navigator and bomb aimer had to be present for the first half hour. The Bombing Leader again warned of 'creeping back'. We didn't know that a few weeks earlier, at RAF Scampton, a cookie had gone off whilst being loaded and had wiped out six Lancasters and most of the ground crew. This illustrates the dangers of the job even before take off. It only needed one incendiary bullet, such as a 'flaming onion' and everything went off. I witnessed this many times. Luckily, I didn't know any of this until later, by which time I was fairly hardened off. Our navigator was given the route to the target which deviated three times to deceive

Squadron Commander begins a briefing (courtesy of Imperial War Museum ref: CH2677)

the Hun and hopefully would keep the German fighters guessing and away from us until the last possible moment. The rest of the crew joined us and the RAF policeman closed the door on us for secrecy but also to stop anybody who arrived late. It was a serious offence. The rest of the crew received their own information. The met. man gave us details of what to expect weather-wise especially wind direction and speed which was important for me. The Intelligence Officer gave us his report and then the CO entered. We all stood up as usual. He told us Pathfinder aircraft would be marking the target for us and the marker colours. The Master Bomber's call sign would be 'Hookey One' and he would let us know what colours were being used by his backers-up over the target. Markers would be replenished every four minutes. The Master Bomber would be circling the target below us, watching and directing as the raid built up, telling his backers-up where to place their markers and instructing us where to aim our bombs. Most of the Pathfinder crews were on their second or third tour and were highly decorated. Little did I think that on my next operation, two days later, that the Master Bomber would be awarded the Victoria Cross posthumously. He was a South African, Captain Edward Swales.

This first operation was the consummation of many hours of flying training and for crews on their first trip it spelt the difference between success and failure. Losses of bomber aircrew in their first five missions were very heavy. In fact, the average number of operations for a Lancaster crew before meeting disaster was just five.

The hours before take off were very busy for the bomb aimer, making sure that everything was set up. The nearer to take-off the greater was the feeling of apprehension, which increased as you collected your gear and got onto the crew bus. Well seasoned crews would be talking and joking; the new crews silent with their nerves stretched. As you climbed aboard the aircraft and the door was slammed shut, stomachs tightened as you went about your checks. Engines were started up, the aircraft moved for take-off and with take-off completed you felt less tense. Now there was work to do.

With the briefing over, the CO stood up and asked if there were any questions; there were none and so he wished us good fortune and said, 'I wish that I was coming with you.' There was a slight murmuring of, 'Bloody liar!' to which he smiled. In fact he had already completed two tours – 60 operations – and was only allowed to fly once a month.

Next, we collected our flasks of tea and sandwiches plus a bar of chocolate and some hard-boiled sweets, then our flying suits, parachutes and harnesses. It was late February and very cold and so I wore a white sweater over a heated jacket which plugged into the aircraft's electricity supply. Two wires ran down to my heated socks in my flying boots. I was wearing 'long john' underpants as well. I put on my Mae West jacket and then my parachute harness, but leaving the straps slack. Once in the aircraft it had to be very tight because, if you had to jump and it was too loose, you would be speaking in a high pitched voice for the rest of your life!

Take-off

Preparations for the flight had already taken three hours. On board the bus to our aircraft everybody was quiet. Ron, our only smoker, was having his last fag for seven hours. At the aircraft the ground crew was waiting with the Salvation Army tea van manned by volunteer women. They were brave women standing right next to aircraft loaded with fuel, bombs and ammunition. As we drank our tea in the dark – no lights allowed – the Flight Commander arrived, asked if everything was all right, jokingly asked if we had the MO on board and then wished us luck before driving off to the next aircraft.

It was time to board the aircraft. Taffy, the pilot, asked me to shine the Aldis lamp down the bombing hatch to show a beam of light for taxiing forward. Aircrew may have had a reputation for being a bit sloppy on the ground but

The Sally Army mobile canteen (courtesy of The Salvation Army)

Lancasters queuing to take off (courtesy of Imperial War Museum ref: CH6095)

when on flying duties discipline was high. For instance, if the pilot ran off the runway when taxiing forward for take-off and got bogged down, holding up the following aircraft or even caused the squadron to call off the op, then the whole crew including any officers would be sent on a discipline course to Sheffield for five days. This was a commando-type course: up at five in the morning, marching with full pack and plenty of menial duties. This was why Taffy wisely asked me to show the way with the light!

The back door was slammed and locked. A Very light was fired and the take-off formation started. There were about 20 aircraft from our squadron on this op and as we were the junior crew, we were the last to go, about 20 minutes after the first plane. At last we were given the signal to start the engines and go. Taffy started each engine in rotation and then called through the side window, 'Contact starboard inner.' As the engines coughed into life, the mechanics unplugged the accumulator batteries and took the chocks away. I switched on the Aldis lamp and we moved forward, queuing for take-off. It was 19.30. Once one aircraft climbed off the runway, another started rolling. We approached the control caravan and when it gave us an Aldis lamp green flash, Taffy used full throttle and gained speed. When the throttle levers were moved up to the 'gate' there was a thin wire across to stop them going further for normal take-offs. For extra throttle you could push the throttle lever through the wire which would break. This would only be done in exceptional circumstances. If you came back with the wire broken, you had some explaining to do for thrashing the engines. The WAAFs from the caravan gave us a wave as they always did no matter what the weather. As we reached take-off speed, we lifted off, the wheels came up quickly, we started to climb. It would take nearly an hour to get to flying height. We headed for Mablethorpe where all the aircraft turned for Germany. This was why timing and keeping to specified heights and speeds were so important. When you had anything up to 500 aircraft on a raid, collisions were the last thing you wanted. The navigator gave Taffy a course to steer and speed to fly which was entered into the log.

An aircraft in flight is subject to the wind like a ship on the tide. Flying directly into a wind of 60 knots with the aircraft airspeed indicator at 200 knots then the aircraft would be covering the ground at 140 knots per hour. The strength of winds vary at different heights, often 100 knots at 25,000 feet. Wind speed and direction cannot be predicted. So conservation of fuel was very important as you were only given just enough fuel plus a small reserve. Many an aircraft crashed coming in to land due to lack of fuel.

The raid

Having reached our flying height of 16,000 feet, we were wearing our oxygen masks. Ron told Taffy to alter course and adjust airspeed. He had worked out that we would be over the target a little early. There was still an hour to go. Taffy was using 'George'. Ron was working hard, getting a fix every six minutes on the 'Gee' radar making sure we were on course and on time; he was also plotting ahead so that if the wind altered he would know and issue corrections.

The searchlights were up, feeling about the sky; some spasmodic flak – flaming onions, the lighter type of anti-aircraft fire – dropped away short. I supposed that I was the only member of the crew that had seen this before, living just outside Dover during the early part of the War. We altered course once more toward the target and Taffy called out that he had picked up the target some 50 miles ahead. Ron told me to put on the bombsight computer and noted this in his log, then he set about preparing a course for home after which he was free for a while. I told Taffy that I was moving down to my bombing compartment at the front. I picked up my small oxygen bottle, took out my oxygen pipe from the main supply, plugged in the bottle, pulled out my intercom lead and signalled to Reg, our flight engineer, that I was coming past. Once in the bombing hatch, I plugged in my intercom, unplugged the oxygen bottle and plugged into the main supply, then I let Taffy know that I was all set up. He acknowledged and I called to Ron, 'All bombs fused' which he logged. All the bombs were then live and all the computer and bombsight switches were on.

The flak was now coming thick and fast. We could feel explosions all around. I was the only one with a panoramic view of the target. As we closed on the target, I was the only person talking over the intercom with the pilot repeating everything I said. I started to push the 'window' out but then asked if Reg could come down and take that over.

Being the last of the squadron to go in, the target was well alight and 'creeping back'. So the Master Bomber called up his backers up to drop green markers which lasted about four minutes to stop the 'creeping back'. The target seemed to be a long time coming into the bombsight. I called for, 'Bomb doors open' and Taffy obliged. The wind rushing through the bombs was very eerie. At that moment a twin-engined aircraft went across under me and I said to myself out loud, 'Didn't know we had twin-engined aircraft on this op.' Straight away, Micky, the mid upper gunner said, 'You bloody fool, that was a German fighter, I've been watching him!' A few moments later, he fired off a burst of gunfire and the fighter cleared off.

While this was going on, the rest of the crew were 'heavy breathing.' I continued with the bombing run, gave a correction and then pressed the bomb

Duisberg with fires still burning after an 18 hour RAF raid
(courtesy of Imperial War Museum ref: C4707)

tit and called, 'Bombs gone!' The aircraft rose a little, I kept the bomb doors open so that the aircraft would fly straight and level to allow the overlap photos to be taken, then, 'Bomb doors close.' There was a sigh of relief from all the crew.

I hadn't noticed that the flak had increased. It was coming thick and fast. This was the Ruhr; Germany's strongest defences were here. We were now out of the target area and turned on our course for home. I looked back over the target and thought, how did we get through all that?

We dropped to 10,000 feet and took our oxygen masks off, taking turns to use our tea flasks and to eat our sandwiches. I saved my sweets and chocolate for Ed. We headed straight for home, encountering some more flak. Soon after leaving the Dutch coast behind, we arrived over our base and called up for permission to land. We were stacked up. As there were five or six aerodromes around Lincoln, controls were very strict to avoid collisions. Even so, there had been several in recent weeks. Everybody kept a sharp look out until it was our turn to land. We landed safely and went to our parking place, switched off the engines, collected our gear and left the aircraft. Ron, standing well away from the aircraft, took huge drags on his fag. We had been airborne for about seven hours.

It was only when I collected my parachute that I realised that during my bombing run in the front of the aircraft, I hadn't taken my parachute with me

Debriefing by the Intelligence Officer: What was the flak like? Any fighters? How many kites did you see go down? (courtesy of Imperial War Museum ref: CH5310)

and as I had to kneel on the only exit from the plane in flight, I couldn't have got out! I made sure I got it right in future!

The crew bus arrived with the other crews already on board. I hoped that there were no crews missing. Most of the lads were quiet. First we handed in our flying kit to the WAAFs in the store, then we went to the main debriefing room. 'Well done, lads,' said the CO as the WAAFs handed us coffee with rum. We waited to see the Intelligence Officer with his WAAF shorthand typist taking down all our answers to his questions, anything unusual etc. I had to report to the Bombing Leader who asked questions about the raid and was satisfied. Then the whole crew went to the mess for the customary egg and bacon.

All the crews had returned safely. There wasn't much talk, we were all very tired. We finished our meal, collected our bicycles and went to our billets. We just about took our clothes off before flopping on to our beds and falling asleep.

Promotion and Aussies

Our hut orderly woke us up at 9am. It was now 22 February 1945. I always liked to get up straight away to get the best of the hot water. Some of the others did the same. Ron and Sid were always last. Ron always looked like a walrus when he woke up with his 'air force' moustache. He was the oldest in the crew at 26. I washed and shaved, made my bed, tidied up my locker and then with Pat, Reg and Mickey went to breakfast on our bikes. We had good food in Bomber Command compared to some other services. I suppose we were a bit pampered. We had sheets on our beds and our laundry was collected and returned weekly. As we entered the mess, we noted that the Battle Order was up and we were on it. Briefing was to be at 1400. The mess filled up. As we were new we didn't know too many people but I noticed that there were four Australian crews, so Pat would be all right with some of his countrymen. The Aussies were a good hearted lot but as mad as March hares. They would bet on anything: flies crawling up the window, cockroaches and certainly guessing the next target. All our crew ate breakfast together, except for Taffy who had been promoted to Flying Officer and therefore used the Officers' Mess. I had been promoted to Flight Sergeant.

After breakfast I went to the Bombing Section and was surprised to see Flying Officer McMahon walk in. He was a Canadian that I did my training with at Picton and Rivers. I always called him Mahoney which I found easier to say than McMahon! We greeted each other with some dry cracks. The Bombing Leader told us to go out to our aircraft. There were no modifications, so Mac and I went off and he introduced me to his crew – all Canadians except for his

Cuban pilot whose name was Encisco Y Siegle and became known as the Cisco Kid. They were quite some crew.

All our crew met at the aircraft and carried out our inspections. There was a full fuel load of 2,150 gallons. I watched the 4,000lb bomb plus 16,000lbs of incendiaries being loaded – the others left before this started! Then I went back to the mess for our last meal before take-off.

Afterwards we sat around in the lounge getting to know the other crews. The Aussies had received large parcels from home. One of the Aussie bomb aimers had been sent a sheepskin waistcoat and, as I was admiring it, he asked whether I liked it and I did, 'Well, if I don't come back, you can have it' he said. A week later, he and his crew went missing and I was duly given the coat. That was the way of things on an operational bomber squadron. After the War, it was used as a pram cover for my daughter.

An unexpected night off

It was briefing time. The target was Pforzheim, a small town between Karlsruhe and Stuttgart. I wondered what was there. Just after the briefing started, the Flight Commander came in and told us the operation had been scrubbed. So, with an unexpected night off, we got dressed up in our best blue uniforms and took the bus into Lincoln. We had a good night. Pat, Sid and Mickey took to English beer. I wasn't a big beer drinker, neither were Taffy and Reg. We all went easy on the drink anyway, because if you had a hangover and were sick into your oxygen masks whilst flying you were in big trouble!

Next morning, we were on the Battle Order again. After breakfast, I went to the Bombing Leader for briefing and he said to me, 'Right, I'm going to the CO and I'll be about an hour. You're in charge.' I looked at him and laughed. 'I'm serious,' he said, ' There's the chair, sit in it,' and off he went. A bomb aimer came in, an officer, and he saluted me, a flight sergeant. So I asked him why he was saluting me. 'Whoever sits in that Leader's chair represents him and you salute whoever it is,' was the reply. I thought that I could get used to that! The Bombing Leader returned and I pushed off. The fuel and bomb load was still on the aircraft from yesterday.

Pforzheim

At the briefing we heard that the target was still Pforzheim which was very strange. It was very rare to have the same target after it was scrubbed. There had to be something important there. We were also flying in the night fighter area – some of the German night fighter pilots had notched up over two hundred bombers each! The belly of a Lancaster, where none of the gunners could cover it, was fairly easy prey.

After briefing, we went through the usual routine: collected our gear, went out to the aircraft, Ron had his fag, we drank our Salvation Army tea and had a quick chat with the flight commander. It was still light and we expected to be over the target at dusk. We boarded the aircraft, the door was slammed and locked, one by one the engines were started up, the chocks were taken away, we taxied out following the line of aircraft to the caravan. Our turn came, we turned on to the main runway and waited for the green light, our signal to take off. Taffy pushed the throttles up to full, the aircraft picked up speed, the WAAFs waved, we lifted off the ground and slowly started to climb with our heavy load. We headed for Reading, by that time we had to be at our flying height of 10,000 feet which was quite low. It wouldn't be very healthy! We turned to cross the Channel. I went down to the bombing hatch, asked Taffy to open the bomb doors and to waggle the aircraft about in case there were any loose bombs in the bomb bay. This was so that any loose bombs would drop into the Channel and not on some poor squaddie in the front line. Events were moving apace on the ground with Allied troops pushing into Germany. I looked through the bomb bay; everything was O.K. As it got dark, we kept a look out for fighters. I was

Threee Lancasters in flight (courtesy of Imperial War Museum ref: CH12353)

standing in the front gun turret with guns cocked and ready to fire. Searchlights started to move around the sky and the light flak started to thicken. An aircraft in front was caught by the searchlights and was twisting and turning. Taffy had to alter course a little; Lancasters all around pushed their throttles up, the flame traps on the engines were getting very red; everybody wanted to get clear. A night fighter moved in for the kill and pumped shells into the illuminated aircraft with the rear gunner replying with .303 bullets. It was no contest, the Lancaster caught light, rolled over and blew up; I felt the blast.

With the target coming up fast, I moved to the bombsight. No oxygen was needed at 10,000 feet. Ron gave me an up to date wind, I set it on the computer and told him all bombs fused. He logged it. The flak was very thick. I could see the Master Bomber down below getting really plastered. He was at about 5,000 feet – not a pleasant job! He instructed us to bomb the red markers. We went in and dropped our bombs, flew straight and level to take the overlap photos, heavy breathing from the crew and then, 'Bomb doors close.' By now we were getting the full treatment from the flak and planes were going down around us. Taffy turned for home as quickly as possible.

We soldiered on with a few fighters still about. I was getting tired, so I took a wakey, wakey tablet. We had been flying for six hours. Nearing the Channel, I went back to sit with Ron, opened my flask of tea and ate a sandwich. I asked Ron if he had had a look over the target. Taffy joined in the conversation and said, 'He did come out for about a minute, took a look and said, "Bugger this," and went back to his desk, pulled his curtains and shut himself in!' We landed safely, went through the usual debriefing performance, had our egg and bacon and went to bed. Bed was wonderful.

Next morning, I looked at my bombing photos and they looked good. The target had been a ball bearings factory. We had lost a few aircraft. News of the Master Bomber was a bit sketchy. Some weeks later, we heard that he was badly hurt, told his crew to bale out, tried to bale out himself but was too late. This was the South African, Captain Swales, who was awarded the posthumous VC.

Mannheim

We took off at midnight for factories on the outskirts of Mannheim. This time the Pathfinders were using 'Wanganui' bombing as there was cloud over the target. They would drop marker flares suspended on parachutes above the clouds and we would have to bomb the markers, through the clouds on to the target. However, these markers tended to drift with the wind and so the Pathfinder backers up would constantly change marker colours, notifying us every time because the bombing pattern of the big cookie was a bit unpredictable; it didn't matter about the incendiaries, because the bigger the spread the better.

On the run up to the target we shoved the 'window' out to confuse the AA guns. The explosions formed a cube effect and when you looked as you went in, it looked formidable, but when you were in the middle of it, it didn't seem so bad; then, on the way out and looking back you wondered how you survived. The journey back was uneventful and we landed after six and a half hours.

Cologne

It was 22.00 before we got to bed and we were hoping for a decent lie in, but our orderly woke us at 06.00 and told us there was a flap on. Up we got, washed and shaved – you had to shave no matter what the hour – and cycled to the mess. The Battle Order was already up with take-off at 11.30 and we were on it. We sat back for half an hour after our breakfast and then we started our preparations. We had a change of aircraft: ULN which managed to complete 113 operations by the end of the War. The armourers had been up all night loading the aircraft. It was a huge bomb load: the usual 4,000lb cookie plus 16 500lb high explosive bombs. From the fuel load my guess was the Ruhr. At the

Attack on Cologne (courtesy of Imperial War Museum ref: C4748)

Devastation in the Cathedral area of Cologne (courtesy of Imperial War Museum ref: CL2169)

briefing we discovered the target was Cologne. Our ground forces had not yet reached the Rhine. We had to bomb the city, not the bridge which our troops would need intact. Unfortunately, Cologne Cathedral was within the target area. This was a big raid and our first daylight operation. It was important to be at the correct height and on time ie. within two minutes of our allotted time both for the success of the mission and for our own safety. This was a comfortable op, if such a thing existed! There was the usual heavy flak and I could see hundreds of Lancasters around us. I told Mickey to keep a sharp watch above us; I didn't want some silly sod dropping bombs on us. There was a cover of dust and smoke over the target as I went through the bombing procedure. As soon as I called, 'Bomb doors close' we got out of the area and enjoyed an uneventful flight home. When we reached the Lincolnshire coast we were stacked up, waiting for the call to land and keeping a good watch for our own aircraft and for any German fighters patrolling the coast waiting for easy pickings. We landed safely.

Chemnitz
We had the next day off, but the following day we went on a cross country flight to brush up on our bombing by radar which Ron and I would have to use. We

had another day's rest and then we were on the Battle Order again, our fifth op in ten days. This time it was a very long trip: Chemnitz. With the war drawing to a close, we were supporting our ground forces on some raids. We were all getting a bit edgy. Looking back now, I know that I didn't realise the pressures on us then. We needed some leave, but there was a job to do and that was it.

With the Russians approaching Berlin and us bombing close by, we were issued with small Union Jacks to wear round our necks so that, if we had to bale out and the Russians caught us, they wouldn't mistake us for Germans. Some of our crews had been shot mistakenly by Russians already.

We were a little lucky on this op. We deviated on the way in, flying at 14,000 feet with our oxygen masks on. We had to have the oxygen but it was mentally and physically tiring and it lasted for nine and a quarter hours. Ron kept us on course and on time . We were in the centre of the bomber stream which was much better than being on the fringe where you were more likely to be picked off. I started the bombing procedure amid the usual heavy flak. After 'Bombs gone' the photos would only be pictures of the marker flares, just to prove that we had been there, as there was a layer of cloud over the target. We headed for home as quickly as possible to save fuel. Reg had to switch over to the emergency reserve fuel tanks with still some way to go, but we made it thanks to careful husbanding of the engines.

By the time we had eaten our egg and bacon, most of the crews were back except for the Cisco Kid crew. We went to bed and were allowed to sleep in until about midday. What bliss after being so tired. The Cisco Kid crew had returned and I asked what had kept them. They laughed but I bet they were not laughing the previous night! Apparently, their bomb aimer, my friend Mahoney, had overshot the target and didn't drop his bombs on the run in, so they went round again which was like committing suicide. To do this you had to turn and head back against the stream of bombers and then turn into it and have another run up to the target. Not only was this extremely risky but extra precious fuel was used which was why they were so late back. On your own, there was also the risk of being picked off easily by the fighters. Mahoney, being the officer in the crew, was not popular!

Dessau

We were on the Battle Order again with take-off at 17.10 for another long trip. Our target was Dessau. As I got into the aircraft, Ron told me that the pee can was in another aircraft. I went over to the hangar to get it and called up to the mechanic for it. He appeared with it and said, 'Is this it?' as he dropped it some 20 feet. Unfortunately, there was some pee in it and it went all over me. I could have killed him. I had to have a good wash and get changed.

We were to use 'Wanganui' bombing again which was not very accurate but effective for mass bombing. With a long trip ahead we all took wakey, wakey tablets. We met fighters and heavy flak as usual. Dropping the 'window' out of the plane, I held on to the loop of string as long as possible which ensured that the metal strips were sprayed over a wide area confusing the German radar and gunners as much as possible. To overcome this the Germans covered the target with a cube box barrage. There were three main types of anti-aircraft fire. Flaming onions were tracer shells and came up at you like a string of sausages but at 10,000 feet or above would not bother us too much; however, if you had a problem and flew below that, they were dangerous particularly if they hit a box of incendiaries when the plane would just blow up. Medium ack-ack gave off a yellow flash; heavy flak gave off a blue flash and was lethal. With all that coming at you, the bomb aimer had to lie there and do his job with only a quarter inch of metal and perspex to shield him. I called, 'Bomb doors close,' and we turned for home. The trip lasted almost nine and a half hours and it was 0200 by the time we got to bed. Within five minutes all was quiet except for some gentle snoring.

Kassel

Nobody wanted to budge when our orderly woke us up at 09.00. Slowly we gathered our wits, washed, shaved, dressed, cleaned up our bed spaces which were in a mess and then cycled off to breakfast. Once again, we were on the Battle Order with take-off at 17.00. We were getting operation weary. We had taken two doses of wakey wakey tablets the previous night and they took a while to wear off. We drank plenty of tea with our meal. In the Bombing Section I had a moan to the Bombing Leader who understood but said jokingly, 'Serves you right for volunteering!' I helped supervise the bombing up. I had the greatest respect for the armourers: one mistake and we were all goners. The target was Kassel, yet another long trip.

After take-off we climbed to our height slowly with our full bomb load. When we reached our flying height the sky was clear and we were leaving trails behind us making it easy for the fighters to find us. We hoped that the searchlights wouldn't find us because with a full bomb load we wouldn't be able to throw the plane about to shake them off. Ron gave me a fresh wind speed and direction when the target was sighted and I moved down to the bombing hatch and started the usual procedures. The flak was fierce; other bombers had baffled the German radar so we were getting the cube barrage flak. There were Lancasters all around; ahead, one exploded and we felt the blast; parachutes soon appeared. All my concentration was on the bombsight. The wind speed and direction that Ron gave me was a bit out, so I had to give frequent corrections. I kept the bomb doors closed as long as possible, but then called, 'Bomb doors open.' As they opened, I heard the familiar eerie sound of the wind rushing through the fuselage coupled with the heavy breathing of the crew on the intercom. The 4,000lb cookie went first and then, ten seconds later, the incendiaries. After 'Bomb doors close' we dropped to 10,000 feet still being hassled by searchlights and ack-ack but we got home safely after eight hours.

Our crew

With a night off, Ron, Pat, Sid and Mickey went into Lincoln again; Reg and I stayed in the mess. He didn't drink at all and I wasn't a big drinker. Taffy came to the mess to see me. The Flight Commander had suggested that, as Taffy was the only officer member of the crew, that there should be another officer and so he asked me if were interested. I said that I wanted a few days to think about it. In the last few days some of the crew had been getting very edgy, the pressure was beginning to tell. Taffy and Ron had been niggling each other and, at times, I had had to patch things up. I certainly didn't want the crew to split up when we were well on the way to completing our 30 ops tour of duty. I think Taffy

Our crew, 576 Squadron, Fiskerton
Dickie Parfitt (Dover), Reg Grout (London), Sid Witt (Toronto), Ron 'Taffy' Burnell (Wales),
Pat Mumford (Australia), Ron Watson (London), Mickey Lobzinger (Vancouver)

wanted somebody to keep the peace. He was in a difficult position; although he came out with us sometimes, perhaps he felt left out of the crew and needed somebody to lean on – after all, I was the ripe old age of 23!

Our crew had very different backgrounds. Taffy Burnell was 22, Welsh, had left grammar school at 18 and joined the RAF at 19½. He had not experienced the world of work and with a dour personality was not a good communicator, but he was very clever and a first class pilot. Ron Watson, the oldest crew member at 26 was a Londoner. He had worked in a surveyor's office, hence his very good navigation. His wife was expecting a baby. Ron had a strong personality and dominated Pat, Mickey and Sid to a certain degree. Pat Mumford, the wireless operator, was from what he called a small farm of 400,000 acres in New South Wales. He was easy going with a pleasant personality and with a fairly easy life he never had to worry much. Reg Grout, the flight engineer, was young without much experience of life and was not a good mixer. He had a girlfriend and lived on the outskirts of London. Mickey Lobzinger, the Canadian mid-upper gunner, was very vocal and outgoing and very generous. His father owned a newspaper in Vancouver and I suspect that he had an easy life, probably out of touch with the real world. Sid Witt, the rear gunner from Toronto, was used to the backwoods. He was a first class shot, self sufficient and mischievous.

Then there was me. I was born in 1921 and went to Elvington School. I started work at 13 years 10 months at Tilmanstone Colliery down the mine on shift work six days a week. I had to walk half a mile underground once I went

Dickie at Elvington School in 1930

Dickie with Bob McCarthy and Eric Broadbent, 1936

down the 500 foot shaft. I was given the job of door trapping which was quite dangerous. The coal face chamber had doors to retain as much good quality air as possible from the smaller ventilation tunnel alongside. The door trapper had to ensure that the doors were closed as much as possible but had to open them to let the coal trucks in and out. I worked at it for six weeks before training another 14 years old. Two weeks later, he was crushed to death. His name was Billy Moore, from Ashley, and he is buried in Waldershare Churchyard. I had the benefit of the community life of the village of Elvington – both the bad and the good! At 14 I was playing football in a man's team and cricket at 15. I was thrust into adult life with all its responsibilities at a very early age. Perhaps that was why I could cope with Taffy and Ron, until I became exasperated with both of them and gave them a good, old-fashioned, miner's telling off!

To continue the story, Taffy and I went down to the village pub where we met up with the Cisco Kid and his bomb aimer, my friend Mahoney. They were pushing me to go for a commission. We went back to our billets at a reasonable hour as we were expecting to be on the Battle Order next day, possibly on a daylight raid. Most of the others were still out on the town. At about midnight they returned making a noise waking everybody up. Sid did his usual trick of shoving a bullet into the combustion stove making a bang and a mess. I said to myself, 'I'll fix you sods!' Next morning we were woken up early and so we assumed we were on a daylight raid. Sid came across to my table at breakfast with a big grin. I said, 'You'll be sorry!' He was a likeable lad of 21, full of mischief.

Essen

We were on the Battle Order with briefing at 08.00. It was a full bomb load with high explosives not incendiaries. The target was Essen. I wasn't looking forward to this one. The Ruhr had a ring of anti-aircraft guns and going in at 16,000 feet wouldn't be healthy especially in daylight. It would only last five or six hours but we would need to keep a good look out. The met. man advised that there could be cloud over the target so Wanganui might have to be used. The Intelligence Officer warned us to watch for rockets and the CO. told us it was a big raid. The ground crew were still fussing around when we went out to the aircraft. We were getting to know them well; they were good lads.

With quite a few crews who had completed their tour of 30 ops and others who had gone missing, we were now halfway up the list for take-off. With only 20 aircraft from our squadron on this trip we were soon off the ground, waved off as always by the WAAFs. Taffy called me to the front and asked, 'Did you check that the bombs were stowed properly?' I had left it to the armourers. Taffy

Dropping 'window' during a daylight attack on Essen (courtesy of Imperial War Museum ref: C5634)

was concerned that the aircraft had swung quite a bit on take-off. I thought it could be due to having a full load of high explosive bombs for the first time. At 17,000 feet I had to remind the crew to put their oxygen masks on. Sometimes I nearly had to force Ron to put his on. We couldn't afford him to go ga-ga. Over Mablethorpe I left the navigator's cubicle and looked around the sky. It was full of Lancasters, obviously a very big raid. The cloud thickened up and, as expected, the Master Bomber called to tell me to use Wanganui. Soon it was time to start my usual bombing procedure. I started 'windowing' and then dead ahead some silly sod had dropped his bombs on another Lancaster and had taken a wing off. The crew were baling out as the aircraft wallowed and then disappeared. This was not unusual on large raids especially at night.

As I called, 'Bomb doors open' I could feel the flak explosions and bits of shell hitting the fuselage but I completed the task, called, 'Bomb doors close' and we turned for home. Dropping through the cloud, it was raining and visibility was poor but at least there was no flak nor fighters about. Being a fairly senior crew now, we shouldn't have to stack up before going in to land; however, as Taffy was about to call for permission to land, another aircraft called for permission. It was already on the landing circuit; it was the new crew, the last to take-off. We had to go round the circuit again. Taffy was very cross but I told him that the Flight Commander would sort out the other pilot. He was a flight lieutenant who had been in Training Command for some time, hence his rank, and had rather a high opinion of himself. He was about to learn that, in Butch Harris's air force, you didn't buck the trend. At debriefing the Engineering and Navigation Officers were waiting for him. They asked for the engineer's and navigator's logs and then took the pilot into an office. After checking from the logs what speeds had been flown, we could hear them tearing strips off the pilot. He emerged looking very dejected and was lucky not to be demoted. He had obviously been flogging the engines.

With debriefing over, we had the usual egg and bacon then had a night out in Lincoln. We persuaded Taffy to come with us. Everybody seemed fairly happy but we didn't stay out long. We could be on another daylight raid the next day. It was now 14 days since our first operation.

Dortmund

We were not woken up, so we all went to breakfast at about 08.00. Our mental clocks were all over the place with the different times that we went on duty plus

100 Lancasters on a daylight raid (courtesy of Imperial War Museum ref: C4552)

the effects of the wakey wakey tablets. It didn't help our patience. We looked at the Battle Order and we were on yet again with briefing at noon and take-off at 13.15. At least we could have a leisurely breakfast and then sit in the mess lounge which we hadn't done for days. We chatted to some of the new crews. Pat felt at home with the new Aussies, a right Bolshie lot. He had previously been with another crew and had had to bale out over England and so had received an Irving caterpillar badge that he was very proud of.

We made the usual preparations. The bomb load was a cookie as usual plus 16 500lb high explosive bombs again. The Armaments Officer showed me the reason for not being able to tighten down the 500lb bombs and hence making the aircraft swing on take-off; they were made in America and were a different shape to the British variety. The target was Dortmund. The Flight Commander was on this operation, standing in for a sick pilot. He was also taking the pilot of a new crew for familiarisation. We were warned of strong winds for the return journey and so it was even more important to conserve fuel. Despite being a bit frayed at the edges – in 20 days we had been on eight operations, a cross country exercise, a bombing practice and two training sessions in the decompression chamber – we completed our preparations and went out to the aircraft. We had to use a different aircraft as our Z Zebra had taken a pasting on the last trip. When the Sally Ann tea van arrived we had just one mug of tea. It was best not to have too much to drink, having a pee at 16,000 feet into a gallon tin in the freezing cold is not recommended!

A new broom

A new flight commander arrived and informed us that he was not impressed with our behaviour on the ground, especially the Aussies, and had decided that when not flying we would parade for an hour each morning. We all turned out for parade the next morning including the officers and NCOs. The ground crew had a good laugh. Some of the Aussies refused to take part and were hauled before the Flight Commander. From what we heard, the Aussies didn't mince their words. Apparently, Butch Harris got to hear of this and called the Flight Commander for an explanation. There were no more parades. I can only assume that Butch Harris was not having his 'old lags,' as he called us, humiliated.

Nuremberg

Our next operation was another long trip: Nuremberg. We took off in the dark at 17.35. I used the Aldis lamp to guide us. As we would be flying right through the German fighter zone in southern Germany, we would have to make a few alterations to our course on the way in. It was not so easy to fool the Germans now. They now had radar which was not affected by 'window' and the Junkers 88 aircraft had improved radar detection units on board. Unmanned rockets were now being launched into the bomber stream from the ground but at this time were not capable of homing on to us, thank God. When that happened, it could easily wipe out most of our bombers. Some of these rockets had been shot down by our crews but could not be claimed as 'kills.' In daylight jet fighters were beginning to appear. The Germans were also using a device to damage our morale. Into an anti-aircraft shell were packed small parachutes and when it exploded it gave the impression that an aircraft had been hit and the crew were baling out. These 'spoofs' looked real enough from a distance.

Once over Reading we set course for Germany. Before flying through the fighter area I moved down to the front guns as agreed with Taffy. It was a bit uncomfortable with no seat in the turret; I had to stand astride. I set the guns for firing and searched the sky. Ahead were many Lancasters, thickening flak, searchlights and fighters. Some aircraft were blowing up, others were going down with some parachutes or perhaps they were spoofs. I could see the target ahead. The raid had started. I moved down to my bombsight and started bombing procedures. I could see the glow of the flame traps all around us. The gunners were keeping a sharp look out. There was so much activity and the target was well alight. Pat was working 'fishpond' to identify fighters from bombers. The Master Bomber called up, 'Bomb the green'. He was down below controlling the raid – rather him than me! This was the worst raid I had been on and I couldn't wait for it to be over. I picked up the target in my bomb sight, called, 'Bomb doors open,' picked up the bomb tit, gave one more direction correction, the target appeared in the centre of the bombsight, I pressed the tit and called, 'Bombs gone.' The cookie went, I counted to ten and the incendiaries followed. Waiting for the photos to be taken seemed like hours, but eventually I called, 'Bomb doors close.' The heavy breathing stopped and we turned for home once again. I needed a wakey, wakey tablet after that and, once we reached France with no flak, we took turns to have our tea and sandwiches. I went back to sit with Ron. He was relaxing after working flat out. We had been flying for seven hours. I noticed that Ron had used the pee can and now I needed to use it, replacing it in a safe place. Mickey, the mid upper gunner also wanted to use it, so I took over his turret for a while. Jack of all trades, that was me! Sid, the rear gunner, had the luxury of the aircraft's Elsan. Crossing the Channel meant that we were only an hour from base. The lads were sucking their boiled sweets. As I always saved my sweets and chocolate for Ed, I pinched a sweet from Reg.

We landed safely. Everybody was eager to get out with Ron gasping for a fag as usual. The ground staff asked if we were all right and then checked the plane over; there were plenty of holes and a few gashes in the fuselage. After returning the gear to the clothing and parachute stores, we enjoyed our coffee and rum and sat down together in the debriefing room. The Intelligence Officer asked about the trip. I said, 'Quite a lot of spoofs,' and he replied, 'They were our boys, not spoofs.' We had lost quite a few Lancasters.

When the crew debriefing finished, he interrogated me on my own as usual. I remembered as much as I could but I was feeling very tired, the tablets were wearing off. He didn't push me too much and when he was satisfied that I couldn't give him any more information, he told me to buzz off or words to that effect.

Whilst eating our egg and bacon in the mess, another crew came in. The rear gunner, Flight Sergeant Brooks, sat with us. Drinking a cup of coffee, it rattled in the saucer. His nerves were frayed. They had had a bad flight and had lost an engine as well as gaining a few gaping holes. Brooksy was all right after a few beers! The Cisco Kid crew came in; they had had a few problems too. With our meal finished, we cycled back to our billet, where the fire was going well, and flopped into bed. We could do with some leave.

At least we had the next night off with yet another trip into Lincoln where we had a drink and went to a dance. We didn't stay long but returned for an early night. Our orderly called us at 09.30. There was no Battle Order up but we were not allowed out which meant that there might be something on.

After breakfast I went to the Bombing Section. The Bombing Leader greeted me with a wry smile and introduced me to a newcomer to the squadron. 'I've a job for you,' he said, 'take our friend to the hangar and show him any modifications to the aircraft. Don't forget to show him how to release the cookie manually.' He laughed, remembering a previous occasion when somebody had been shown the manual release procedure and a 4,000lb bomb had dropped onto the bomb doors! I had had this job to do several times and I always looked through the bombing hatch window first to see if any bombs had been left on.

Back at the mess, the Battle Order was up and we were on it with take-off at 00.15. The new crew's pilot would be joining one of the experienced crews to be blooded. Brooksy was having a last pint; this would be his last operation of the tour. I suspected that he would want to come back for a second tour. Some people were playing cards, most put their feet up in their billet. I decided to go back to the billet. The mail had arrived. We made good use of the waiting time by writing letters, putting our dirty washing out and changing our bed linen. Some pressed their 'best blues' hoping for some leave.

Another long trip

Taffy sent a message asking us to be at the aircraft at 13.30. The fuel load was the maximum, 2500 gallons, which meant another long trip. Whilst talking to the Armaments Sergeant, I rested my hand on a bomb, but I whipped it off quickly. It was so hot that it almost burned my hand. He looked at me and laughed. The bombs had been standing in the sun all day! 'Bugger you,' I said and left him to get on with it! With still another hour to go before briefing, we had a sweep on the name of the target. I plumped for eastern Germany.

High in the skies over Germany in temperature way below freezing, we fought the night fighters equipped with .303 machine guns against 30mm cannon fire. The sky was a big place, whilst some of our aircraft would fall prey to the fighters, the majority would get through. Throughout the War it was a continuous struggle with both sides constantly changing tactics. Usually visibility was poor but, when it was good, we would leave vapour trails, giveaways to the fighters which would have easy pickings on such nights. To survive, strict coordination by the crew, practised on fighter affiliation exercises at base, was essential.

It was a long trip and we all went to sleep quickly afterwards.

Hanau

Next day, the target was Hanau with a target time of 03.30. The Intelligence Officer told us to expect fighters particularly as we would be leaving trails. We would be flying in at 20,000 feet. The Met. Officer confirmed that we would have clear skies and light winds. The Engineering Officer gave us the usual warning not to flog the engines on this long trip. We would be using oxygen for most of it. This helped all the while you were using it, but once you stopped using it, tiredness and depression set in and you would take a wakey, wakey tablet to counteract it which helped for a couple of hours. By then, hopefully, you would be back at base, ready for sleep. On our eleventh operation in a month and desperate for some leave, we were at a crucial point in our tour. With the average life of a Lancaster being five operations, we were well over the limit and pushing our luck.

At 22.00 we left the mess after our meal; Taffy was waiting for us and we all boarded the crew bus out to the aircraft. We didn't have to hang about long now for take-off as we were about third in the queue. As we climbed up to 20,000 feet, I told the crew to put on their oxygen masks; lack of oxygen could easily creep up on you and before you knew it, you could be out cold. Mickey, our mid-upper gunner was always vocal and told Taffy about aircraft above us. Sid, our rear gunner, didn't say much usually, but on clear nights he kept us informed about our own aircraft around us; there was safety in numbers, provided you didn't get too close to each other. There were fighters about, but we were in the centre of the bomber stream and hopefully safe. Being in the front of the raid, I wouldn't have the benefit of the leading aircraft bombing and lighting up the target. I would have to rely upon the markers which only lasted four minutes. Ron advised me that the target was 35 minutes ahead.

Later, Taffy called to say the markers had just gone down, so I unplugged my oxygen mask and intercom, moved past Reg down to the bombing hatch, put all the switches on, fused the bombs, gave Taffy some course corrections, got the markers in the bombsight, called, 'Steady,' and then, 'Bomb doors open.' The target reached the cross in the bombsight, I called, 'Bombs gone!' As usual I waited for the photos to be taken and then called, 'Bomb doors close.' Ron had already set course for home. Once we left the target area, I manned the front gun turret, but having no seat up there, I soon moved to my seat at the navigator's table. After five and a half hours flying and one wakey, wakey tablet I was desperately tired, but so close to home I didn't want to take another tablet because I wouldn't sleep when we got home. A drink and a sandwich helped to keep me awake.

I was desperate for a pee. I looked for the can and found that it had been used already by Reg and Taffy; it was quite full. It reminded me of when I was very young, living in Somerset. We had an outside lavatory and so at night we used a chamber pot a lot. If one of my three brothers had used it and I was in full flow, it was a bit difficult to stop when the pot was full; Mother was always complaining about it. I called up Taffy on the intercom and told him and Reg to get their own tin before the next op.

Crash landing

By now, we had reached the coast and were picking up other aircraft heading for home. Taffy spotted one of our squadron with one of its wheels dangling; it looked as though it had been hit. It was one of the Aussie crews. As we were over the sea, Taffy decided to escort them home.

The pilot, a 21 years old pilot officer, had to make a choice. He could either fly around to use up his fuel, then ditch near the shore; or, he could use most of his fuel, head for Carnaby or Woodbridge and attempt a crash landing. Those two aerodromes and Manston were equipped to take any aircraft in trouble. He opted for Woodbridge and we left him at the Essex coast. We landed straight away as soon as we reached base. The busy flight had lasted seven hours.

As usual, the ground staff greeted us with, 'Any problems?' Apart from a few holes in the fuselage, we told them we needed an extra pee can!

At the debriefing we were told that the Aussie crew had crash landed at Woodbridge with no injuries and were now on their way back. The young pilot had been recommended for a DFC.

After breakfast, we soon headed for our billet and flopped into bed. We went into Lincoln that evening. Taffy came with us and told me that he was disappointed that I didn't get a commission. Pat had been promoted to Warrant Officer Grade 1 (WO1).

Our orderly woke us at 07.00. After the usual morning chores, which included taking my best blue trousers from underneath the mattress in an attempt to restore a good crease after our night out, we cycled to breakfast. The Battle Order wasn't up, so hopefully we would have some time off. Taffy wanted to see us at 10.00. We were to do some practice bombing using H2S, the navigation bombing aid and the gunners were to practise in their turrets firing air to sea. We were up for three hours. A bit of a waste of time, I thought.

We got back at 17.00, had a meal, changed into best blues and went into Lincoln. We had a couple of drinks and some fish and chips from the chippy halfway up the hill to the Cathedral. We had been warned not to be late back.

Bremen

We were woken at 05.30 and realised that there was a flap on. We were briefed at 0630. The target was a heavily defended oil refinery north of Bremen. The Americans had gone in the day before and had not done very well. Just our squadron was going at 10,000 feet with a cookie and 16 500lb high explosive bombs. Take off was at 08.15. So, it was all a bit of a rush and a daylight raid that we weren't used to. The briefing was quick: expect fighters, heavy flak and some cloud. At least it would be a shortish flight, but on the return journey we would pass over Kiel Harbour which was also heavily defended.

It was 08.15 on a cold March morning. Pushed for time, we ate our meal quickly, cycled to the flying clothes section, collected our gear and boarded the bus to the aircraft. Ron saved time by having his fag on the bus. He had been busy for the past hour working on his charts. The ground staff were still milling around. The Armourer Sergeant and I checked the bomb load. Last aboard, I signalled to Taffy who closed the bomb doors and off we went. We were now second in line for take-off and with a very heavy load we didn't dare stray off the runway. We lifted off successfully and started to climb. We levelled out at 10,000 feet. This time we wouldn't need oxygen masks. With 50% cloud I might have to use the H2S, so I checked that it was OK. It would be another hour and a half before we reached the target and so I went up front with Taffy and Reg. I noticed that there were some Lancasters from 617 Squadron tagging on to us.

They could only carry one bomb, a ten tons 'tallboy;' they were so big that the bomb doors had to be taken off to accommodate them. After a while they changed direction and moved off. We wondered what they were up to. Later, we found out that they had bombed the Eder Dam.

My lucky day

With half an hour to go, I went back to Ron at the navigator's table who gave me an estimated wind speed for my bombsight. This could be a visual run up although the Pathfinder Master Bomber was in charge. I didn't want any cock ups. I started the bombing procedure. As I saw the target ahead in a bend in the river, I could feel the explosions around us. The markers went down and I lined up the aircraft, gave another correction and called, 'Bomb doors open.' At that moment, I heard a loud bang. We had been hit. I carried on with the run up, but I could feel liquid in my eyes. I wiped it away and saw that it was blood. I

Lancaster over the Bremen oil refinery, 21 March 1945
(courtesy of Imperial War Museum ref: C5101)

Line overlap photograph of the Bremen oil refinery by Dickie Parfitt, 21 March 1945

couldn't feel any pain so I continued the run, gave more corrections and then, 'Bombs gone.' After 'Bomb doors close,' Taffy asked if I was all right. 'I don't know,' I replied. Blood was coming from my forehead. With so little room in my bombing hatch, I climbed back to the cockpit where Reg checked me over. I was cut above the forehead. For once, I didn't have my goggles down over my eyes. Reg then spotted two holes in the right shoulder of my battledress but I couldn't feel any pain. Taffy handed me a piece of flak about the size of a half crown which had hit him in the leg but had lost its strength against his flying boot, so he wasn't hurt. He kept the piece of flak as a memento.

Flak was fierce as we passed south over Kiel Harbour but we moved on over the North Sea. Taffy called up base, reported me injured and got clearance to land first. As we touched down we were followed by the 'blood wagon' and the station fire engine. As soon as we parked I was first off and the medics were waiting for me. By now I was wondering what all the fuss was about. Nevertheless, I had to lie down on the stretcher and was taken to the medical centre where I was given the full treatment. My face was patched up and my eyes were cleared of perspex dust. When they took off my battledress they found two holes in the right shoulder of my blouse, two in my sweater, two in my shirt, my vest was torn with just a scratch on the skin underneath! I could only assume that the flak that had hit Taffy's leg had come up through the perspex of the bombing hatch where I was crouched over the bomb sight. With all the clothes that I had on, it had gone through the front of my shoulder clothes, out the back and up on to Taffy's leg, dropping at his feet. On the bombing run up the aircraft had drifted down a starboard track; if the bombing run had been slightly less to starboard, my right shoulder would have been taken off. It was my lucky day.

I was taken to the debriefing centre where the CO and the others were keen to know what had happened. We were given seven days leave immediately; our money and rail tickets had been specially arranged already. The lads said that I should get injured more often! I went to the clothing section to get a new battledress top but the officer was right snotty about it and refused to let me have one. So I asked to phone my flight commander and told him what had happened. 'Put the officer on,' he said. I can only guess what he said, but I had my new top in less than two minutes!

Leave at last

After a meal I got changed, packed a few clothes plus the chocolate and sweets for Ed, caught a bus with the others into Lincoln and then the train to London. My face was patched up and I was wearing sunglasses. The civilians were looking at me and the lads were laying it on thick. The civilians couldn't believe that at 10.00 that same morning we had been over Bremen. In London we went our separate ways. I told Sid to be careful about what he picked up. I reached Dover Priory in the early evening, climbed all those steps up from the station to Priory Hill and down the other side into Tower Hamlets, turned into Dickson Road and knocked at the door of number 15. This was Ed's mother's house where Ed was living some of the time. Ed came to the door and was surprised to see me. I hadn't had time to let her know that I was coming home. We had a bite to eat and then went home to our flat.

Next day we took the bus to Elvington to see my mother. She was worried when she saw me still patched up but I calmed her down and we took our favourite walk down to the woods where I had played as a boy. I remembered lighting fires, baking potatoes, playing cowboys and indians, fixing up tents in the trees, in the summer picking wild strawberries and in the autumn collecting chestnuts and baking them – not to mention playing conkers. Looking back, they were wonderful days. We strolled back to Mother's where, despite rationing, she always managed to put on a good meal.

Back in Dover Ed and I with Ed's mother and father went to the local pub. As I entered the bar, some sailors stood up and saluted me with my patched up face and dark glasses. Ed and I often laughed about 'being a hero.'

The leave went all too quickly but we went to the pictures and to a couple of dances at the Town Hall where Freddie Overton looked after us well. That was where I had met Ed when playing in the band for him. It took me back a couple of years when I was playing at one of his dances and a shell hit the back of the Town Hall. All the lights went out. There were nearly a thousand people there, servicemen and women as well as locals. The officials wanted to clear the hall but the crowd asked us to keep playing which we did. They probably thought they were safer inside than out on the streets. To this day I feel that the people of Dover and the part Dover played in the War has not been given enough recognition: the evacuation from Dunkirk, the Battle of Britain, over 2,000 shells plus bombs, land mines and doodlebugs. There were also the miners down the four pits who never knew whether the winding gear would be hit with them a mile or so underground starving of oxygen. After using oxygen when flying high and the decompression exercises, I could well appreciate their situation.

My face began to heal after a few days and the irritation in my eyes cleared. I went with Ed collecting insurance money, sometimes way out into the country. When the War ended, the insurance men would get their jobs back – if they came back.

Ed saw me off at the end of my leave and I met up with the rest of the crew at King's Cross. Pat, Sid and Mickey had had a good time in London. It was all new to them. Ron, from north London, had seen his daughter for the first time. Reg had got engaged. Taffy had been home to Wales.

Hamburg

Back at base we were woken up by our hut orderly. I looked at my watch: it was 03.45! There was a flap on. We washed and dressed quickly. Ron was not at his best in the morning at the best of times. I could hear him moaning and groaning. We did not stop to make our beds but dashed off on our bikes. We had no bike lights and were stopped by a special constable, 'You can't ride bicycles without lights,' said he. Crew were piling up behind us, then the Aussies came and almost ran the stupid man down. He stepped aside and we carried on.

In the briefing room we were told that the target was Hamburg with a load of twelve 1,000lb bombs and six 500lb high explosive bombs. After the briefing there were no questions; it was too early for the brain to be working! We were dismissed by the CO. with the usual, 'Wish I was coming with you.' A few new crews had joined us to replace those lost and tour expired.
Our aircraft was dear old Z Zebra which was already bombed up with guns loaded. On board I looked at the bombs. This was the first time we had carried such a load. They all had different falling speeds which complicated matters. I would be using the 'Mickey Mouse' switch which was for stick bombing – my first time at that caper.

We were first to take-off. Once we were on our way, Taffy told me that the aircraft had swayed a lot more than usual but there was hardly any wind. He wondered whether the bombs were properly secured. I had checked and they looked all right. Over the sea, we opened the bomb doors and waggled the plane about but no loose bombs fell out. We left it at that. I told him that with these bombs I would need a longer bombing run and the bomb doors would have to be open longer. That wouldn't please the lads.

Don't panic

Ron wasn't very happy with the performance of the main compass halfway down the fuselage which supplied the Gee (navigation aid) and H2S. It was playing up. So he asked me to go back and check it, but with the target coming up soon I asked Pat, who was nearest, to do it. Usually I was the only one to use the small oxygen bottles when moving about the aircraft and always checked that my bottle was full. The others stayed plugged into the mains supply. Pat grabbed the nearest bottle to him, plugged into it and clambered over the main spar of the aircraft to the compass. We waited to hear from him over the

Hamburg after a raid (courtesy of Imperial War Museum ref: CL2500)

intercom but heard nothing. Eventually, I decided to go after him and plugged my oxygen bottle to my mask. I found Pat slumped on the other side of the spar, sparked out. There was no time to mess about. I took off my mask, gave him a few whiffs of mine, he revived a little, I took a few whiffs myself and then gave him some more. I put my mask back on, helped him back to his seat and plugged him into the mains supply. After a few breaths he was OK.

Taffy was getting anxious with the target coming up fast. I told him everything was all right now and would explain later. I took up position and started the procedure. With a layer of cloud the target couldn't be seen and so the markers were dropped and floated above the cloud on their parachutes. After a few corrections I released the bombs, waited for the photos and called, 'Bomb doors close,' much to the relief of the crew. I hadn't noticed the thick flak we had endured for the last half hour. A Lancaster quite near us had gone down on fire, another was in trouble and the crew had baled out. Mickey counted them all and recorded the aircraft letters to report at the debriefing – if we got there ourselves.

Ron gave Taffy a course for base, we descended to 10,000 feet and took off our oxygen masks. I stood in the front gun turret and put the guns on to 'fire'. There were fighters about.

Once over allied territory we relaxed a little and had something to eat and drink. Approaching the Lincolnshire coast, Taffy was about to call up base for permission to land when another aircraft beat him to it. We listened to his call sign; it was one of the new crews. They were given short shrift by the controller and were told to stack up and wait their turn. They would be in trouble later. We were told that there was fog at base and FIDO would be used. We picked up the airfield, entered the funnels (the normal lights that guided you to the runway) and went down the tunnel of flames to land. I thought about what would happen if a tyre burst and we swivelled into the flames. We wouldn't have a chance. We landed safely.

Taffy insisted that the oxygen bottles were checked. Pat had flaked out because he hadn't checked his small emergency bottle of oxygen and it had leaked away over time. After debriefing Taffy, Reg and I cornered the Armaments Officer and asked about the high explosive bombs that we were now using. He told us that they were American, slightly different in shape, and there would be a slight movement all the while we carried 1,000 and 500lb bombs. British bombs would be all right.

As usual we headed for the Sergeants' Mess for our meal and poor Taffy had to go to the Officers' Mess on his own. We changed into best blues and headed for Lincoln. We took our ground crew with us and lent them our battledress tops. They thought they could pull the birds better dressed that way! We all had a good night.

Next morning with no Battle Order we all had a leisurely breakfast with a bit of time to socialise. We met the new crews. As a senior crew you had a certain standing with them; they regarded you with some respect which did the ego good. I moved on to the Bombing Section and had a good gossip.

The news was that the War was not expected to last much longer. I hoped not! More sophisticated weapons were being used against us. The night fighters now had homing radar fitted to them controlled from the ground.

We had another decompression exercise. We agreed that Pat should take his mask off first. He sat down and started writing on the pad. After a minute his writing got scrawly, his speech was slurred and after another few minutes he flaked out. The instructor put his mask back on and after a few puffs he was back to normal. We all had our turn. Some went off faster than others. We needed to relax after that and spent the evening in the local.

In at the deep end

Next day there was no Battle Order, but our crew had to go to Grimsby for dinghy training and in the afternoon had a trip on the air sea rescue launch. Dinghy training was in the swimming baths. First, we each had to put on a bathing costume, battledress, Mae West, shoes and dark goggles and then each man had to jump off the high diving board into the deep end on his own. A dinghy, upside down, was already in the pool and had to be put it the right way up single-handed. First it had to be found, which wasn't easy in dark goggles. Once the person had done it, he signalled to the rest of the crew with his whistle. He had to keep blowing it so that they knew where he was – they were also wearing dark goggles and were dressed similarly. We all took a turn, simulating ditching in the sea at night. We always wore these whistles on our battledress on the front of the collar. People always asked us what they were for and the girls would say, 'Can we blow your whistle?' There was no answer to that!

After a packed lunch we went to the harbour and boarded the air sea rescue launch. I had seen them before in Dover Harbour. They were nearly as big as an MTB (motor torpedo boat) and had two Rolls Royce Merlin aircraft engines which made them very fast. We went into the cabin. The lads couldn't understand what all the padding around the sides was for. The officer said, 'Wait and see.' We set off slowly across the harbour but once outside he opened the throttles. These boats were capable of about 40 knots and so as soon as we hit the waves we were thrown about. Without the padding we would have been

Bombing up for a raid (courtesy of Imperial War Museum ref: CH6103)

injured. The boat was soon turned round and we returned to harbour. That suited us well!

We were back in time for our evening meal and had the night off but were not allowed off base, so we spent an hour or so in the mess and then went to bed. We were not woken up by the orderly, so we took our time getting to breakfast. The Battle Order was up and we were on it with briefing at 16.00. We had a leisurely breakfast swapping yarns. I had a moan about the American bombs to the Armaments Officer but there was nothing he could do about it. We just had to grin and bear it. I went with him to our aircraft to watch the bombing up.

Bombing up

Bombing up procedure began with the bombs being placed on a trailer towed by a small tractor called a tug, sometimes driven by WAAFs. Near where the aircraft was parked there would be an open-ended large building. In there the armourers would fit the fuses and the pronged forks that would prevent the bombs going off prematurely. This was a dangerous job and certainly not one to be over confident about. When a bomb was hoisted into the bomb bay, a wire

Bombing up with high explosive for a raid (courtesy of Imperial War Museum ref: CH12541)

would be attached to the pronged fork. The end of the wire was held by a solenoid which was controlled by the bomb aimer in the bombing hatch. Over the target the bomb aimer would fuse the bomb and it would be fully armed. When the bomb was released the solenoid would retain the fork with the wire attached, leaving the small propeller on the bomb fuse to unwind in the wind on the way down. When it hit the target the striker pin would go home and the bomb would explode. If you returned with all your wires and prongs missing, your bombs would have dropped safe, not armed, and you would be in trouble. This was why I always called to Ron, 'Bombs fused,' and he recorded it in his log. I never had any problems.

Lutzkendorf

On this operation we would be carrying a cookie and 10 500lb high explosive bombs. These were the American type and I could see that they were not a perfect fit when 'crutched up'. We were using a different aircraft, so I went to Z Zebra which was in the hangar having an engine change, and retrieved the pee can! It was a maximum fuel load so we knew we were in for a long night. The target was Lutzkendorf, an oil refinery. The flak was very heavy over the target. Pathfinders did the marking. We were well up front and so we went in and out before the hornet's nest got stirred up. The passage home was uneventful but I manned the front gun turret for the last hour in case German fighters were waiting to pick us off as we reached the Lincolnshire coast. They had even managed to pick off a Lancaster as it landed. We got back at about 06.00.

Helping the Dutch

After about six hours sleep we had lunch. Afterwards, the Bombing Leader, Taffy and myself had to report to the Squadron Commander. Taffy and I didn't know what was up. The Bombing Leader didn't say a word. We entered the hallowed office, saluted and were invited to sit. Then we were told what it was all about. The Dutch people were in desperate need of food and were near starving. Churchill had been asked for food months before but could not supply enough aircraft. Churchill had given in and asked Butch Harris for help.

The Squadron Commander had chosen us, as the senior crew, to experiment with dropping food. It had to be done quickly at a very low height otherwise the food would break up if dropped at more than 250 feet! 'Right ho, gentlemen, get on with it,' he concluded. Thanks very much, I thought.

Back in the Bombing Section we discussed the problem. The bomb doors took about 10 seconds to open. Using the bomb sight at 250 feet we would be miles past the target when the food hit the ground even at low speed. Anyway, we dreamed up some sort of hand-held bomb sight and the Bombing Leader and myself went to the Carpentry Section. After a few hours the carpenter had made the bomb sight. The next day we arranged to experiment with it. We had about a dozen sandbags pushed up into the huge bomb compartment of our Lancaster, which was a bit tricky as the bags had to be held whilst the bomb doors were opened and then quickly closed once they were pushed in. It was too late to do anything more that day. The lads couldn't believe it when we told them what we had been up to.

Ron, Pat, Sid and Mickey all went into Lincoln for the evening while Reg and I stayed in the mess and had an early night. The lads came back at a reasonable hour but woke the rest of the hut up as usual with Sid doing his normal practical joke with the .303 bullet in the combustion stove. I vowed once again to find a way of fixing that sod! Next morning I woke Sid up with a full glass of water in one hand and an empty glass in the other and poured water from one to the other near his ear. In a short while he had to get up and go to the urinal.

After breakfast, it was time for the practice bombing with the makeshift bomb sight. I could foresee many problems and I knew that Taffy wasn't happy flying at 250 feet or less with the Germans and their AA guns still in Holland. We assembled at the aircraft. Control had warned everybody to keep clear of the runway. We took off, climbed to 250 feet, went into the country for a few miles and then turned back to go down the main runway. I had chosen the last intersection as the target. We went belting down the runway at 250 feet and at 150 knots per hour. At very low levels the ground seems to go past very quickly. I held the bomb sight in my hand, focussed it and judged when to call, 'Bomb doors open.' The sandbags fell and landed way past the intersection and splattered all over the runway. I was thinking, 'not very successful,' when I heard Sid laughing. He said, 'Take a look down,' and there were two civilian airfield workers pedalling like hell towards the airfield entrance. Apparently they had not been told about the exercise but then saw a four-engined aircraft flying low down the runway dropping sandbags all around them. They were not happy!

After we landed the Bombing Leader asked for my opinion. I suggested that we dispense with a bombsight of any kind and just use common sense, but that we should have some hooks made so that the sacks could be fitted to the bombing solenoids and then released like bombs. This would make it more accurate. The ground crew had already stuffed the bomb bay with another dozen sand bags so we tried again without a bomb sight but the result was the same.

In the afternoon we had a fighter affiliation exercise. A Spitfire met us and we practised being attacked by it. Our gunners had cameras instead of guns and, needless to say, the Spitfire didn't fire at us! Taffy had to throw the Lanc. about in set procedures and we hoped that the wings wouldn't drop off. It was a good job we didn't have a big lunch!

Kiel Harbour

After a night off we were on the Battle Order again next day. With briefing at 15.00 it had to be a night op. The bomb load was different: a 4,000lb blockbuster plus 16 500lb semi-armour piercing bombs that I had not used before. This was something special and a fairly short trip judging by the fuel load. This had us guessing. At the briefing we were told that Kiel Harbour was the target. Harbours that take battleships are not healthy places and we were going in at 10,000 feet which was not good for survival chances.

We were now leading the squadron and took off first. Ron estimated three hours to reach the target and as we would be approaching from seaward there shouldn't be any flak on the way. Being first meant that we wouldn't have the benefit of the target being alight already. We would have to rely on the Pathfinder markers and so it was important not to arrive early but on time and on track. If we arrived early, before the markers were dropped, we would have to go round again and the crew would lynch me.

Raid on Kiel Harbour: capsized pocket battleship 'Admiral Scheer'
(courtesy of Imperial War Museum ref: CL2772)

Approaching the target I made my usual preparations. The flak was very hot, flaming onions, light and heavy stuff, searchlights. We were getting the full treatment. It was a long run up with the wind coming straight at us, the lads were breathing heavily, just one more direction correction and then, 'Bombs gone.' Being high explosives they all went together. I called, 'Bomb doors close' as soon as the photos were taken and we headed for the open sea. We had the luxury of landing first. Before we got off the plane the ground crew were inspecting for damage but there was nothing serious. By the time we had eaten our flying breakfast it was 02.30 and we soon flopped into our beds. We were told that Pathfinder Mosquitoes would go in at daybreak and photograph the target, so we were woken up at 09.00 and soon headed for the mess. Pinned on the notice board were photographs showing that we had sunk the pocket battleship, Admiral Scheer. It was upside down in the harbour. No wonder the flak was hot. Everybody was chuffed.

We then had three days rest. Our ground crew invited us to go into Nottingham with them. Having repaired it, they had 'borrowed' the Flight Commander's car and had 'managed' to get a tank full of petrol. Reg and Taffy weren't interested but the rest of us agreed to go. Once again the ground crew asked to borrow our battledress tops again. Sadly, Taffy, being the only officer, seldom came out with us. Mickey and Sid were due for their WO1 promotion but I had four months to go. Pat already had his. We had a good night in Nottingham, returning in the early hours. With no Battle Order the next day we were allowed to sleep in. I pottered about and wrote letters to Ed and Mother. Pat had a bit of a cold and I got him some aspirins. Like the rest of us, he wanted to get the tour of 30 ops over and we were more than halfway there now. The odds on surviving were shortening with every op.

Cuxhaven

We were not called the next morning, but later in the day the Battle Order went up and we were on it. Doc Henderson visited Pat and put him in hospital. One of the main reasons Pat was not to fly was the rarefied atmosphere at 20,000 feet or more. If your breathing wasn't too good, it could cause problems. Sometimes, when we descended after dropping our bombs, we heard Mickey screaming with pain. He had nasal problems but wanted to go on and finish his tour. If he reported his problem, he would be taken off flying. It was his decision to put up with it and he told us not to worry if he screamed as the pain only lasted for a minute on the descent!

At the aircraft we met the Signals Leader who was coming with us. Taffy had warned us that he was a flight lieutenant with some 40 operations to his credit.

We would have to watch our 'p's and q's.' Our fuel load was low and our bomb load high. This was unusual on a night raid. With the weather deteriorating, I half expected the op to be scrubbed. After our midday meal we flopped around waiting for the briefing. The target was Cuxhaven, another naval base and another risky mission. The CO enlightened us. The whole Operational Training Unit (OTU) with Wellingtons and other aircraft would be going plus the whole Heavy Conversion Unit (HCU) with Halifaxes and Lancasters. None of these crews had any operational experience. The plan was for the OTU to go about 50 miles toward the target and then to turn back. The HCU would go almost to the target and then turn back. This was to give the dreaded Hun the impression that a large raid was underway. Our squadron of 20 aircraft would carry on and bomb the target from 20,000 feet. That was the good news! The main force was to bomb Potsdam in the very early hours of the morning. The theory was that we would attract the night fighters and the Potsdam raid would be nearly over by the time the fighters returned for refuelling. We would be the sitting ducks! The Potsdam raid was important. We were one of the few aerodromes with FIDO and the CO hoped that the weather would clear in time. I murmured to Ron that I hoped the op was scrubbed.

We collected our flying gear. The weather was closing in as darkness fell and we heard that the OTU aircraft had been called off. The short runway was being used as we always tried to take off into the wind which assisted lift off. We were in front again. Taffy said that it would be a bit tricky with a large bomb load. Picking up speed on full throttle, we hit the runway intersection at take off speed and just lifted off the tarmac. Taffy was struggling to heave her off. The wheels touched the runway slightly, then we were off and started a slow climb. We had all been silent; now we could breathe freely.

After climbing to our height we set course. The wireless operator told us that the HCU had been recalled as the weather had closed in over their aerodromes. Our squadron was now on its own and soon we were in full cloud flying on instruments. I was working H2S which was not much use over the sea. Sighting the Dutch coast, I picked up a fix for Ron and we were on course and on time. Reaching the northern coast of Germany in thickening cloud, fighters were about trying to locate us, dropping their flares all around. They were working in pairs with one above dropping the flares silhouetting us for the plane below. Our plane had no guns in the belly which was 'as bare as a badger's arse.' Taffy told our gunners to keep quiet unless attacked. He wanted to creep through unnoticed if possible.

Nearing the target, I moved to my cramped bombing position. I decided not to use 'window' as there were so few of us on this trip. Ron told me that we were over Wilhelmshaven naval base which explained why things were so hot. Taffy altered course for the target and the flak lessened a little. At last I picked up a Pathfinder marker and told Taffy to prepare for the bombing run. After a few more minutes, 'Bomb doors open.' I could see the markers faintly through the cloud. 'Left, left, steady, steady,' I called to Taffy as the markers moved down the bomb sight, then, 'Bombs gone.' We waited for the photos to be taken with the flak coming thick and fast and fighter flares dropping all around us. As soon as I called, 'Bomb doors close' we turned for home and I moved up to the front gun turret. Taffy stayed up at 20,000 feet in thick cloud. After about 20 minutes the flares had stopped and we assumed that the fighters had run short of fuel and were returning to base. I moved back to the navigator's table and Taffy decided to move down to 10,000 feet. Mickey was crying out in pain; Taffy was descending too quickly. He levelled out and we flew on. Over the North Sea we dropped to 6,000 feet and took off our oxygen masks. Mickey had settled down.

I was working the H2S radar and saw a response on it. I gave Ron a nudge and pointed to it on the radar screen. We watched it for a while. It was getting closer and we were both worried. We were over the sea but a ship shouldn't show such a big response. Ron called up Taffy and asked if he could see anything, but he couldn't in the thick cloud. It was getting bumpy. I went up to the cockpit and looked out. Taffy spotted a high black cloud, cumulus nimbus, we were on the edge of it and being thrown around. Ron quickly worked out a course to go round it, so we went south and skirted it. If we had gone into the core of that cloud, we would not have survived.

Now, having diverted, we were low on fuel and had to go on to the reserve. As a precaution the wireless operator warned any other aircraft in the vicinity. Hopefully we should make base but we received a message from base warning that enemy fighters were patrolling the coast line. Taffy asked for permission to land, explaining our fuel problem, and got priority. Many Lancasters had crashed around their base area through lack of fuel. This was just another factor that made life uncertain! At last we could see our base lit up by FIDO which was only used in dire circumstances due to the high cost. We did one circuit and then into the funnels, entered the tunnel that FIDO created and landed safely. Ground crew found only a few holes.

Sid's 'little bit of trouble'
We then realised that we hadn't had our tea and sandwiches but we were all so worn out that we didn't bother; it had been a hectic flight. As always, the first job was to return our flying gear to the Flying Clothing Section. Sid had to tell the WAAFs that his clothes were a bit messy; he had been taken short. This

needs explaining. At 20,000 feet the temperature was sometimes 40 degrees Fahrenheit below, so we had to wrap up well. The rear gunner's position was even colder and so he had extra suits and heating. He wore long john underpants and vest, thick socks, shirt, thick sweater, battledress trousers and blouse. On top he wore a complete heated suit, Mae West jacket, parachute harness fully tightened and flying boots. To get into his tiny turret he had to open two small doors at the rear of the aircraft. With all those clothes on you can imagine the physical effort required to get in. It was impossible to straighten up. On the journey out, an hour before the target, Sid had severe stomach pains just as we encountered fighters. He had to sit there and 'bake it' – his own words! It had been another two hours before we could relax and take off our oxygen masks. Sid was in agony. None of us had a clue about his problem. He then pulled out his heater and intercom plugs, disconnected his oxygen and stepped out of the turret into the rear of the fuselage. He undid his harness, took off his heated suit, took off his battledress top, undid his braces, dropped his trousers, but could wait no longer and messed his long johns. All that he could do was to clean himself up as best he could, get dressed again, return to his turret and sit in it for another two hours! The WAAFs were very good about it, supplied him with clean pants and trousers and found him a room where he could wash himself. Sometime later, I believe he took out the WAAF who helped him. Sid was a strong, silent type but loved the ladies.

At the debriefing we saw photographs that the Photographic Section had rushed through which showed that we had all bombed a few miles out to sea. Possibly the Pathfinders had dropped their markers too late, the Germans had bent the OBOE beam (used in bad weather to pinpoint the target by three radar beams aimed at the target from three locations in Britain; the Pathfinders dropped their markers where they intersected) or the Germans had dropped spoof markers, the cunning devils. Our squadron had lost two aircraft out of 15. Nevertheless, we were told that we had done the job asked for us – to be the sitting ducks. The main force had bombed Potsdam before daybreak. For us it had been a long, futile night and we went to bed dejected.

I didn't know until after the War that Harold Clark, my brother-in-law who lived in River, was a rear gunner in one of the HCU Lancasters. He had been a flight engineer on Catalinas doing many hours of dangerous flying supporting convoys to Russia and in the Atlantic as well as a tour in India before returning to England. His skipper on the Catalinas was Russell-Vick, later Mr Justice Russell-Vick.

We all slept in until noon and then only came round slowly. We were getting mentally and physically tired. Pat was feeling a lot better. After doing our usual chores around the billet, we cycled to the mess for a meal. There was no Battle Order but Taffy wanted to meet us at 15.00. In the mess there was a lot of moaning about the Pathfinders but I said that we had only been the second eleven. The Potsdam raid had been the big one and it had succeeded. Taffy met us and asked us all to have a night out in Lincoln. He also asked me to try to keep Ron sweet as they were getting on each other's nerves a bit. I joked, 'If you buy him a pint, he'll come round!' We had a good, relaxing night out.

There was no Battle Order next day but the Bombing Leader told me that a load of special hooks had arrived for the food dropping, so we went out to the hangar and watched a demonstration of fitting them. It looked as though the idea would work. The bomb doors could be opened in advance and the bags would all drop together, but I suspected that they would sway on take-off. Back at the mess I found that we were on a cross country training flight which would give me the chance to brush up my map reading. We spent a couple of hours over the Fens which were supposed to simulate Holland, but somebody should have known that the Dutch dykes had been breached a long time and a lot of the land was flooded. Back at camp we weren't allowed out for the evening which meant something was on tomorrow. We all had an early night trying to catch up on sleep. We had been flying nearly every day for a month and were getting a bit fragile.

Heligoland

We were called at 06.00 with a briefing at 08.30 for a daylight raid. The ground staff had been up all night and the armourers were loading up. With 1200 gallons of fuel it would be a fairly short trip. The bomb load was 12 1000lb and 4 500lb high explosive bombs. I figured that we would be bombing concrete defences or naval ships. We went aboard to do our checks including Pat who was fit. At the briefing I sat with Ron who had collected his charts. The target was Heligoland, another naval base. It comprised two islands off the north coast of Germany, one with an aerodrome and the other with a fairly deep harbour; no doubt they would be heavily fortified. A small group of Lancs. would bomb the aerodrome 20 minutes before us to keep the fighters down. We would be part of the main force bombing the harbour installations. Clear skies and a light wind were expected. We were to approach from the sea. With only about four hours flying there would be no tea or sandwiches provided! We were still at the top of the pecking order and the Flight Commander who had now done some 50 ops would be coming too. We would be up front with him.

As we went out to the aircraft I looked at Ron who, as always, looked like something the cat had dragged in with his shaggy nicotined-stained moustache and having his last fag. He was a brilliant navigator and kept us out of a lot of trouble. We owed him a lot, although he was a cantankerous bugger at times. The CO came round in his car with his usual, 'Any questions' and, 'Good luck.' The Flight Commander took off first and we followed.

We all rendezvoused over Mablethorpe, altered course and climbed to 20,000 feet. It was a brilliant day. Up in the cockpit I could see Lancasters trailing behind us. As we approached the target I could see smoke from the attack on the airfield. The small force had done its job. We were right on time and could have a perfect run up. I took up my position, did a bit of 'windowing' and started my procedure. I would be using stick bombing so I wound the Mickey Mouse switch back that allowed the bombs to go down in sequence. The flak was hotting up with everything coming at us but no fighters. I picked out the target which was still intact. First I could see a small town, then the harbour with a long breakwater. I gave course corrections as we approached then, 'Bomb doors open,' another correction and, 'Bombs gone.' I watched them on their way down. I thought they were going to fall short but they were smack on. I hit the town with a couple of 1,000 pounders and the rest went straight down the causeway and exploded. I could see the wakes of ships heading for the open sea as fast as they could. As we headed for home and dropped height, I looked back to see the raid building up. There must have been a hundred or so on this op. We settled down to a steady flight home with no fighters to bother us. It had been a spectacular and comfortable trip. At the debriefing we saw some rushed photos. Everybody was pleased with them including the CO.

A 48 hour pass

With a 48 hour pass we all went to London and then went our separate ways. I went home to Dover where Ed was at her mother's. Once again I had not had chance to warn her. Next day, as usual, we went out to Elvington to see my mother and took the walk to Toy Woods. Mother never asked me about my flying and I didn't tell her. She always believed that I would come back. After a good Sunday tea we went to the Crown at Eythorne and finished the evening with brother Bill. He liked to show me off. There were very few servicemen from those mining villages as mining was a reserved occupation. Most of my local mates who had joined the RAF had either been killed or been taken prisoner.

I had to start back at midday on Monday. I warned Ed that I would be doing some important flying thinking about the food drops to Holland and leave would be scarce. Still, the War couldn't last much longer. We all got back to camp on time, even Sid who had his leg pulled about it.

Bremen

We were on the Battle Order again next day. I went down to the Bombing Section and found Mahoney in the Leader's chair with his feet up. I noticed that he had been promoted to Flight Lieutenant and had a joke about it. He introduced me to two new bomb aimers. I said, 'If you think that I'm going to take them down to look over a Lanc. for modifications, you can think again. I have just come back off leave. I'll sit in the chair and you can show them!' After some banter he agreed and then I put my feet up but the Bombing Leader returned and told me to bugger off to do my aircraft checks. Our aircraft had had its engines changed which should make climbing easier. There was a full bomb load for a short trip. At the briefing we were told that the target was Bremen supporting the ground forces. They were on the outskirts of the city moving quickly and could take it before we arrived. If so, we would be recalled and any crew with over 15 ops had to return and land with bombs intact. Deadly silence prevailed. Crews with less than 15 ops could drop their bombs in the sea. Mahoney had gone slightly pale but then shrugged his shoulders. We were carrying the American bombs and so it was even more important to check for loose bombs for our own safety, if we brought the bombs back or, to prevent them falling on some poor squaddie as soon as I opened the bomb doors.

On the way out to the aircraft we were hoping that the raid would go ahead. Landing with a full bomb load could be tricky. It only needed the landing gear to collapse and we would all be in it even if I made the bomb fuses safe. Before reaching the target we received the message that the raid had been scrubbed! Taffy felt quite confident about landing safely. Fortunately, he was a first class pilot. Now that we didn't have to fly over enemy territory, the return trip was uneventful. Back at base we were given permission to land once all the crews that had dropped their bombs into the sea had landed first. The Cisco Kid went in first and we watched with bated breath. Into the funnels he went, half flap, then full flap, hovered slightly then down. We could see smoke from the scorching rubber of the wheels, then the aircraft trundled down the runway.

We were next. Taffy turned into the funnels. He was letting Reg use the throttles and he had both hands on the control. Taffy was calling out the revs. for Reg. We were coming in faster than usual – if we went below stalling speed, that would be it! It was probably only a few minutes, but it seemed to take ages before the wheels lightly touched the runway; the aircraft floated then settled on the tarmac with quite a bump. I held my breath. We carried on down the runway, Taffy applied the brakes slowly, the end of the runway got closer but we stopped short of the end and turned off to allow the other aircraft to come in. I moved up to the cockpit to find Taffy and Reg covered in sweat. Ron joined me and we gave them the thumbs up. We didn't want to go through that experience again! The ground crew gave us a cheer as we taxied to our spot. The Flight Commander appeared and congratulated Taffy. All four aircraft that had to land with their bombs landed safely. With no debriefing to delay us, after the usual meal we got into our best blues and went off to Lincoln. I hoped that this little adventure would bind the crew together.

Berchtesgaden

We were given the next day off, so we scrounged a lift from a lorry going to Manchester and had a good day somewhere different. I had been before but the others hadn't and they might not get another chance. That night we were woken up at 03.00. Nobody was pleased and a few rude words were uttered. Briefing was at 04.00. So, after another quick wash, shave and breakfast it was off to do our checks. Once again the armourers had been up all night, had fused the bombs and loaded them. The Flight Sergeant Armourer came and apologised for the American bombs again. These were the bombs we had brought back from the Bremen trip that had been stored at the end of the runway. In the briefing room the target on the blackboard was Berchtesgarden, Hitler's hideaway home, or more precisely, the barracks. The Bombing Leader warned us that the height of the mountains needed careful attention and, with the barracks in a valley, we would need to take care not to bomb each other. The met. man gave us clear weather and the Intelligence Officer gave us some useful info. The CO told us we would be flying in a group gaggle like geese. The Flight Commander would be flying and leading with his wingtips painted red. We would fly close but not in formation. If any of us saw a German fighter, we had to fire a Very pistol then we would all close in for cover and greater firepower. Mustangs from Fighter Command would escort us. This was intriguing.

We were to cross the Channel over Dover and return the same way. This had never happened before. I wondered whether Ed would see us go over. During the Battle of Britain she and the people of Dover had seen German bombers in regimental formation fly over accompanied by their own fighters above and below them with a few of our fighters taking them on – aircraft, parachutes and bullets flying everywhere. Now they would see hundreds of Lancasters on their way to bomb Germany at 06.30 on 29 April 1945.

With all this in my mind, 576 Squadron Fiskerton took off, climbed to cruising height, crossed over the Thames and into Kent. I had told the lads about Dover; the two Canadians and Pat, the Aussie, were very interested and the others had not seen the White Cliffs of Dover before. On the way out only Sid, the rear gunner, would have a good view but I promised the others a good view on the way back. We would come back – Mother had said so!

We were well up front at 20,000 feet with hundreds of Lancasters all around us. The Mustangs joined us, shepherding the loose aircraft, getting them into line. I had been up in my front gun turret since well into France. Soon we would be crossing over the German fighter zones where they were most active. Somebody fired a Very pistol. The pilots closed in tight and then I noticed out to port a Lancaster on its own. I imagined the navigator saying that he was right and on course or possibly they had engine trouble. As I watched 2 German jet fighters approached the aircraft and took it out. It spiralled down and its bomb load exploded. Needless to say, that made everybody nervous. The gaggle leader ordered everybody to tighten up.

As we approached the Alps, I dropped down into my bombing hatch. The flak had started and was getting fiercer. We were now over the Alps with not a lot of clearance. This was going to be tricky. I would be on the target quickly with no room for error and we wouldn't want to go round again. The Master Bomber was on the air giving me instructions. I called, 'Bomb doors open,'

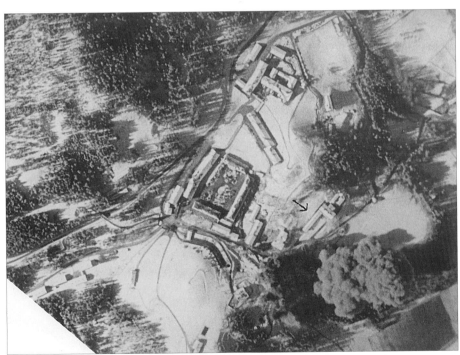

Raid on Berchtesgaden: a bomb burst near Hitler's chalet, 25 April 1945
(courtesy of Imperial War Museum ref: C5243)

suddenly we were there. We weren't far off track, so a few corrections and then, 'Bombs gone.' The flak was coming from everywhere – the valley and the mountain sides. Without the bomb load we soon climbed away and headed back home.

The Mustangs picked us up again whilst we were over Germany but left as soon as we entered French territory. I went up front and stood with Reg as we approached the Channel. We had dropped to 5,000 feet and everybody could move around. We passed over Calais and I gave the lads details of the Dover area. Taffy decided to do a circuit of Dover Harbour. I told him that he wouldn't have done that when the barrage balloons were there. We then flew off north over Elvington, my home village. I had saved some 'window' and showered it on the village after which we headed for base.

We discussed the raid and thought this would be the last as everybody expected that the War in Europe would end soon. This proved to be correct. The raid had taken nearly eight hours by the time we landed. The ground crew were keen to know about the raid but we soon left them to get on with it and boarded the crew bus. We all went into Lincoln for the evening and had a few beers which was a bit of an anti-climax after having been over Berchtesgaden being shot at that same morning.

Operation Manna

Now we had to help feed the Dutch. Between three and four million Dutch in German occupied Holland were facing starvation and 1,000 people were dying daily. Townspeople were foraging in the countryside, eating tulip bulbs and sugar beet and camping in the fields. Something had to be done to avert disaster. The Dutch had risked everything to help Allied airmen downed at Arnhem. Now it was our turn to help them. The British relief operation was called Operation Manna and it ran from 29 April until 8 May, 1945. The Allied and German military agreed to a truce so that the relief work could be carried out; although the drops started two days before the truce was signed! The delivery of the volume of food urgently required could only be achieved by using bombers laden with food. 12 million Red Cross packages were waiting to be dropped on POW camps in Germany and three million were diverted to Holland. 350,000 steel hooks were used in the bomb bays. Initially there were four drop zones each surrounded by German artillery. The Germans checked that food was dropped and not weapons!

We had a leisurely morning. I even sat around in the mess lounge for a while which I hadn't done for weeks. A few of us went out to the aircraft to watch food being loaded. We were to carry 5,000lbs of food crammed into the bombing bay.

Five panniers had been fitted and each pannier held 70 sacks. The trip would be early the following morning so drinking was out that evening but we went into Lincoln to the pictures and had fish and chips afterwards. Back at base we were told that briefing would be at 03.30; however, nobody woke us because the operation was scrubbed due to bad weather.

We had to stay on camp and so Taffy gave me some pilot refresher training on the link trainer. Later, I whiled away the time in the Sergeants' Mess until bedtime. The weather forecast was good for the next day, 29 April.

At the briefing we learned that our destination would be Valkenburg. The dropping zone would be marked by the Dutch and we would go in at 100 feet – very low for a four-engined aircraft. If fired on, we were not to return fire. This was still occupied territory and the Germans could get itchy fingers and I would be right in their line of fire. At least at 100 feet anybody trying to hit us would have to be very quick! The flight should take less than two hours and we would be leading our squadron. There would be a lot of aircraft on this op and some crews had little operational experience. I would need to keep my wits about me. At least it was daylight. I wanted to get in and out quickly!

We soon saw the Dutch coast. Then the 'dreaded Hun' opened up with a short burst. I was ready for the drop and asked Taffy to open the bomb doors. I could see the markers ahead and, 'Thank you, boys,' in front written in tulips. I let the food go; some fell in the water but most fell near the marker. With my job done I closed the bomb doors and we headed for home. We were all quiet. It had made quite an impression upon us. Back at base we were thankful to have something nice to eat. Over the next few days we dropped food on Valkenburg again plus Ypenburg and Terbregge near Rotterdam twice. The last drop was on 7 May, 1945.

Bomber Command dropped nearly 7,000 tons of food with 3,181 Lancaster sorties. The Americans also carried out 2,200 sorties. The BBC and Dutch radio announced the drops so people cheered and waved flags, teacloths and even sheets as we went over. Many aircraft crews made their own small contributions by donating their own sweet rations and throwing them out attached to small home-made parachutes with notes that said, 'Voor Het Kind,' (for the children). There were some hiccups with some bags landing off target, some damaged on landing; margarine was a problem – dropped as packets but converted to flat pats on impact!

The Dutch authorities organised collection, storage and distribution throughout the country. They also decided the priorities: first were the church organisations looking after the sick, the children, hospitals and orphanages. Red Cross 'shops' were used for general distribution. The cooperation of the

Germans was essential but this did not prevent the Reich Commissioner from being hanged for war crimes later. Such was the impact of this operation on both the providers and the recipients that a Manna Association was formed which still maintains close links between the participating aircrew and the Dutch people.

The War in Europe ends

With the European War over, we were given seven days leave and I went home. The shelling had stopped and people were going about their business without fear. Ed and I did the usual things: the pictures, a dance, visited Mother, attended a few fêtes and flower shows. We also bought some second hand bits of furniture. Furniture, clothing and food were still rationed, of course. Ed was still working for the Prudential and we did some collecting together. It was soon time to return to Fiskerton. I wondered what would happen. The Japanese were still at war.

Chapter 5
POST WAR SERVICE

Operation Exodus

Back at camp we had to report to the Flight Commander who told us to fly to Brussels to pick up some prisoners of war and bring them back. My sister, Babs, was in Brussels in the ATS; I thought I might meet her there. The rest of the lads were keen to see Brussels as well. I had been there as a Scout on a camping holiday.

We landed near Brussels and saw these thin and ragged POWs standing about waiting to be flown home. It was a very sad sight for us but we were a grand sight for them! We put about 20 in the fuselage with the few bits and pieces they had. There would be no time to find my sister. We made them as comfortable as we could; we weren't built to carry passengers! I pointed out the Elsan and told them to expect a lot of noise for the one and a half hour flight

Former POWs waiting to board aircraft home (courtesy of Imperial War Museum ref: CL2434)

Former POWs boarding aircraft for home (courtesy of Imperial War Museum ref: CL2427)

home. I stayed with them all the way back and didn't wear my parachute harness because there were no parachutes for them! The noise meant talk was out of the question but some played cards. From time to time I was asked how much longer it would take and I pointed to my watch face. It was an issued American watch for Ron and I. If it varied more than five seconds, we had it checked; such was the standard of navigation. As we approached base I told them to sit tight. Taffy made a good landing. Once out of the aircraft we all shook hands before transport took them off.

The airborne repatriation of POWs mainly from German and French airfields was called Operation Exodus and 74,000 were brought home by 28 May. Runways had to be repaired first. Another problem was how many could be safely carried in each aircraft. Unfortunately, we found out the hard way when an aircraft crashed killing all 25 passengers and 6 crew. Passengers sitting mainly in the rear upset the flying trim and caused the pilot to lose control. Thereafter, no more than 24 passengers were carried and they were carefully positioned. The POWs were provided with newspapers, magazines, cushions, blankets and special rations to prevent air sickness. Sometimes bands played as they landed and WAAFs swamped them with tea and cakes. Transit camps were set up near airfields where they had a bath, a shave, a haircut and were kitted out. They were also given cigarettes – no health warnings in those days – a railway warrant and £5 in cash before they moved on.

Hush hush

Next morning Taffy told us that we were to take the CO, Group Captain Arbuthnot, to Brussels but Taffy would not be coming with us. Most peculiar, we thought. We collected our flying gear and went out to the aircraft, not our usual Z Zebra. We waited for the CO to roll up in his chauffeur driven car and then introduced ourselves. He told us to get on with our checks and he, as the pilot, did his with Reg. With the war over I had none to do! While the engines warmed up I asked Ron what he thought all this was about, but he just shrugged his shoulders. Control soon gave us clearance and up we went. We had never flown with this chap before but it was too late to worry about that! We went up through cloud to about 5,000 feet when it cleared and then flew just on top of it. After about five minutes, the CO called me to the cockpit and told me that he was turning back as the cloud was too thick; he hadn't had many flying hours experience with four-engined aircraft. By this time all the crew were listening on the intercom. He had been flying twin-engined Mitchells and wasn't too happy with Lancs. Ron gave him a course for home. Then the CO asked me to go to the bombing hatch and look for a hole in the cloud to descend through. 'This is getting worse,' I thought to myself. I called up to him, 'A break to port, skipper,' and he promptly stuck the nose of the aircraft straight down the hole. I was hoping that when we broke cloud we wouldn't be too low! However, we came through at a reasonable height, headed for base, did a couple of circuits and landed – quite a good landing, too.

The CO told us to stay on board, got out himself, handed a case to Taffy who climbed on board and took off for Brussels! On the way I told Taffy what had happened and asked what the purpose of the flight was. Either he was bound to secrecy or he didn't know. He had been told to deliver the case to a certain person and then return to base. All very odd!

During the next couple of weeks we did a load of practice flights: radar bombing over York, five hours bombing practice at 20,000 feet, a seven hour flight practising mine laying, a flight affiliation exercise with a Spitfire, more high level bombing and then more flight affiliation. I couldn't see where all this was leading to. Ron and Taffy were getting a bit touchy with one another again and I began to lose patience with them. I told both of them to pack it in, otherwise I would ask to leave the crew. They had another go at each other. I was fed up with being the peacemaker and decided to see the adjutant who was from the Dover area. I put my cards on the table. He told me that the CO would not stand for any quarrelling in his crews and after a week I was posted to 625 Squadron Scampton with a sprog crew. I was sorry to leave the crew; they had all been good at their jobs. Anyway, Sid and Mickey would soon be returning to

Canada and Pat to Australia. Looking back, perhaps we were all feeling the strain and realising what a dangerous job we had been doing. At Scampton I was told that I had been posted there in error and so I was re-posted to 626 Squadron Wickenby.

Wickenby

At Wickenby I joined a crew that hadn't flown any ops and so I was looked up to in a way. After one training flight I wandered down to the gymnasium and introduced myself to the PT instructor and then did some exercises. He watched me then came across. 'You've done this before,' he said. I told him of my days with Cyril Eades at the Barn in Elvington and the displays including the one for King George.

I asked him if there was any chance of a game of football as I had played professional football as an amateur. Apparently the station was in the last eight of the RAF Cup. With no flying for the next few days I did a bit of training, anxious to impress to get into the team. The PTI arranged a kick about with two scratch teams and asked me to play. My captain introduced himself as Reg Flewin – the Portsmouth player and England captain! The game started and I felt comfortable. On the other side was a good player doing all the work midfield; I discovered that he was Frank Soo, right half for Stoke and wing half to Stanley Matthews. They were the quality players that you could come across in the RAF. After the match I was invited to join the station side.

Italy

A couple of days later we had to fly to Italy, just outside Naples at a place called Pomigliano, to pick up soldiers on demob or leave. It was only a few miles from Vesuvius. We had to have some inoculations and were given some large yellow tablets. We were also issued with KD uniform (khaki) but we didn't have time to sew on any badges. Parachutes were left behind so that the soldiers wouldn't be nervous. I had never done that before even when training. It was a straightforward flight of six and a half hours: over France, down the coast of Italy, over Vesuvius and then landing at Pomigliano. The heat hit us as we left the aircraft; it was my first experience of a hot country.

I was in charge of 20 blankets for the soldiers to wrap up in on the aircraft. I didn't know whether to leave them on the aircraft or not but the ground staff sergeant soon put me right, 'Take them to the guard room. These Italians will nick anything!' he said. We were billeted in Portici, near Pompeii, in a small hotel. Meals comprised egg and bacon on continental bread. We were told not to eat fruit without washing it first in a bucket of purple something.

We had a day's rest before returning and so we went into Naples for the evening and walked down the Via Roma. With no identification on our outfits at all, nobody bothered us. It was only when we visited the Sergeants' Mess on the Via Roma and some had too much vino that the locals and our own service police found out who we were. Locals then approached us, wanting to swap our English pound notes for about 700 lira in counterfeit notes to spend in Naples. The exchange was carefully done with both holding out the notes at the same time and both letting go together. It was illegal and our service police were on the lookout for it, so as soon as the exchange was made, the notes were put into your pocket and you nipped around the corner to check it. You would probably find that instead of having one 500 lira note and one 200 lira note for your pound, somehow the 200 lira note had been withheld and you only had 500 lira. By that time the locals had disappeared! We learned the hard way.

A sight that I shall always remember was a Jeep chained to the lamp post by its steering wheel for security, but instead of wheels were four wooden boxes! We were told not to go down any side streets unless you wanted your throat cut! By now small boys were after us offering us their pretty sisters. We walked back to the Sergeants' Mess for a drink and a chat where the army blokes enlightened us into the ways of the people of Naples. An army lorry took us back to our hotel after a long day.

Pompeii

Next morning after a sort of breakfast: cereal, egg and 'dipped' fruit, we went into Pompeii. We went to the church first where the prostitutes were offering their wares outside; there was also a chap selling cameo brooches and I bought one for Ed. We entered the church but had to pay to go in; I wasn't very impressed being brought up in the Baptist tradition. The gold and precious stones in the ornaments and on the walls and ceiling were beyond belief particularly when compared with the prostitutes outside and small children with no shoes begging for food. It's not surprising that I tend to be an agnostic.

We walked on to the ruins of Pompeii and on the way I bought some grapefruit to take home; I hadn't seen grapefruit since the War started. In the main street under the shadow of Vesuvius where the shops had been, I saw shop counters which were worn in places where coins had been scooped up. Young boys came after us for pound notes to change and pestered us for cigarettes or anything else like clothes and shoes. We got rid of them by promising to bring things next time. The better houses had a form of lead plumbing. Carrying on down the narrow street of ancient shops and houses we came to a rich merchant's house; standing by the entrance was a chap who demanded two cigarettes to enter and see some erotic paintings. We paid up and then paid another two cigarettes to see a covered painting. It was called, 'Worth its weight in gold'. He uncovered it to reveal a gladiator wearing armour and a short skirt; his eight inch penis was placed on one side of a pair of scales with some gold on the other side. We all had a good laugh!

Eventually we made our way back to Portici, had a meal and then went to the beach, part of which was reserved for our troops. This didn't stop the prostitutes parading up and down. The crew I was with were very young and were tempted but I told them that they would probably catch VD; that was enough to keep them on the straight and narrow. Some of us went in for a swim and enjoyed it. The evening was spent in the Sergeants' Mess in the Via Roma where a band played 'Come back to Sorrento.' It was the first time that I had heard it; after the War I introduced it at Dover Town Hall when I played with the 'Crotchets'.

When we arrived at the airfield the next morning the soldiers were waiting for us. I collected the blankets and issued them. They were very respectful to me; I was equivalent to a staff sergeant; it was the first time that I had been accorded such eminence. I gave them a talk about what to expect on the flight and pointed out the Elsan. Their faces lit up at the prospect of being back in Britain in six and a half hours after being abroad for several years. The aircraft went straight up and over Vesuvius with our fingers crossed hoping the engines wouldn't fail. As soon as we crossed the English coast I prepared the soldiers for landing at Glatton where they would be processed. Some shed a few tears knowing they were over England. Once on the ground I helped them all out, shook hands with them and then jumped back on board for the short flight back to base.

Broken nose

Arriving back early evening, we cleaned up and had a decent meal. I was given a 48 hour pass so I caught the night train to London arriving home early in the morning. Ed hadn't been up long. She was pleased with the brooch and the grapefruit. We had an enjoyable weekend doing the usual things. At Elvington I arranged to play for Eythorne Football Club at Deal on the Saturday. Halfway through the game, going towards the goal, I went to head the ball and got kicked in the nose which broke. I was taken to Deal Hospital but they couldn't do much with it except to put a plaster on. I got back home late plastered up. Ed wasn't pleased; she had arranged an early birthday party for me. My head was still painful next day so I went to Buckland Hospital for an X-ray; I couldn't feel the back of my head but they assured me the feeling would come back. The broken nose wasn't blocking my breathing so I was sent home.

Only after the Cup

Back at base I was down to fly to Naples in two days time. I went to the gym to loosen up. The semi-final of the RAF Cup was in five days time on Doncaster Rovers' ground and I was playing but I had to tell the PTO (Physical Training Officer) that I couldn't play because I had to fly to Naples; sickness was the only reason for not flying. 'I'll see about that,' he said. In the afternoon I was called to the Adjutant's office and he greeted me with, 'You've upset a few people! The CO will tell you what it's all about.' I hadn't a clue who the CO was until I walked to his office and saw his nameplate on the door: Squadron Leader Blemier-Hasset, my old flight commander at Fiskerton. 'Sit down,' he said; that was unusual. 'You are not flying to Naples, you are playing football,' to which I replied, 'If you say so, sir.' We talked about the old times and I told him that I was getting fed up with going from squadron to squadron, flying with sprog crews. I wondered if I could be made redundant for aircrew. He said that it was possible and told me to see the Adjutant, but only after the Cup run!

The PTO was pleased that I would be playing but I also told him that I had asked to be made redundant and would like him to give me a good recommendation to take a Physical Training Instructor's course. He replied that he would be pleased to, but only after the Cup! As a matter of courtesy I went to the Bombing Leader and told him what had happened; he was not a happy man.

So, whilst the crew flew to Naples, I did some work in the gym and a few laps around the aerodrome to get a bit fitter. On the day of the match the team boarded a coach for Doncaster; I sat with the PTO and talked about the future. He asked if I were interested in staying on in the RAF; he was sure I'd get a commission. I told him about my previous attempt! At the ground we got changed and I learned that not only did we have some international and First Division players, so did the opposition. I was beginning to learn that if you were good at sport, especially football, and you were not aircrew, you could have a good position in the Air Force; perhaps I could have some of it. The game was a bit disappointing; we were beaten by one goal.

Something to declare

I was on another trip to Naples. This time the Polish Air Force was waiting for us in full force and fully loaded. They had bought up everything and were bringing it back to England for some sort of racket. Unfortunately for them, Customs got wind of it and were waiting for them at Glatton!

Elsham Wolds

By now there wasn't much for Lancaster crews to do. The longer serving men were being demobbed and I was posted to Elsham Wolds. I joined a sprog crew with flying officers as both pilot and navigator. The pilot fancied himself and was a bit offhand with me, a mere flight sergeant. We had to do some bomb disposal work, dropping 4,000lb cookies into Cardigan Bay. The bombs weren't fused and in theory were safe but the Bombing Leader told me not to take any chances in case somebody had left the odd fuse in.

After doing my checks at the aircraft, the pilot came to me and asked what I was going to do. I told him that I would need 1,000 feet for every 1,000lb of bomb plus an extra 1,000 feet for safety. I felt that he didn't much like being told anything. The rest of the crew were a bit apprehensive, not having flown with high explosives before. We took off and I sat with the navigator with the curtain drawn using the radar. After a while I could feel the aircraft swaying about. We were 15 minutes from the dropping zone. I got up to go to the bombing hatch, pulled back the curtain and found we were flying at 1,000 feet amongst the Welsh mountains! I tapped the pilot on the shoulder and asked if he would mind flying at 5,000 feet! All the crew overheard it on the intercom; he didn't like that one little bit. I ran through the bombing procedure, looked down and found that we were lower than 5,000 feet and asked the pilot once again to fly at 5,000 feet. Silence, but he did it. Then I asked him to circle the bay to ensure there were no boats about, opened the bomb doors and released the bombs. There was a splash and that was it. I got a very black look from the pilot afterwards.

Back on the ground the pilot asked for a word. 'I don't care very much for your attitude, Flight Sergeant,' he said. 'And I don't care very much for your flying, Sir,' I replied, saluted and walked off!

As usual I reported to the Bombing Leader whom I had known at Fiskerton and told him that the bomb had dropped safely but added that I didn't want to fly with that pilot again. He asked why and I told him. He agreed with me. Anyway the situation was resolved the next day when the Adjutant told me I was being sent on a redundancy course at Catterick. So it was goodbye to flying in Lancasters or any other aircraft for me.

St. Athans

The redundancy course was all about putting square pegs into square holes and after a few hours I was told to proceed to St. Athans in Wales for a PT course. I stayed the night and left next morning for St. Athans. With the War over the railways had improved and kept good time. The RAF station was a big place: an aerodrome plus a PT school. There were a few more aircrew on the course plus some ex POWs who were warrant officers and flight sergeants. We had to parade at 0900 next morning at a big complex comprising a large gymnasium, large cinema and swimming pool. There were quite a few leading aircraftmen (LACs) and ordinary aircraftmen (AC2s) in the squad, young chaps who had not long joined up. As senior NCOs we were processed first. We were greeted by our instructor, Sergeant McMillen, or Mad Mac as we called him. The weekend was coming up so he told us to familiarise ourselves for the next few days and the course would start on Monday.

A few of us arranged to play a football match between ourselves. The instructor laid everything on including a referee. I noticed a squadron leader on the touch line and after the match our instructor called me over to meet this officer. With a strong Scottish accent he said, 'You've played before, laddie. What's your name?' I told him. 'Right Parfitt, I want to see you in my office first thing tomorrow morning.' Apparently he was the CO, Squadron Leader Hugh Brown, and was mad on football.

There were quite a few famous sportsmen instructing on the station: Len Harvey, the British and Empire heavy weight boxing champion, a lot of Welsh rugby players, some pro footballers and Ken Thom, a Walker Cup golfer all of whom had had an easy time during the War. I was to meet many of them during the course.

Next morning I was ushered into a room with about a dozen other chaps, mostly LACs and corporals. I was the only flight sergeant. The CO was at the table. I was introduced to everybody. This was the station football team. There

No. 6 PT Course, RAF School of Physical Training, St. Athans, January 1946

Dickie Parfitt is top right, S/Ldr Brown is seated in the front row, third from the left; Sgt 'Mad' McMillan is seated on the extreme right

were nine First Division players all Scottish and a corporal from North Kent that I was to meet after the War. The team was in the quarter finals of the South Wales Cup.

We started the course. Every morning we assembled in the gym. Mad Mac had been born and brought up in Japan and was a judo black belt. Apparently he had made a service film about how to deal with a bayonet charge with your bare hands. We kidded him that it wasn't possible so he borrowed a rifle and bayonet and we all took turns charging at him. We all ended up on the floor! Hence we nicknamed him Mad Mac.

We did plenty of PT, judo with Mad Mac and rugby. I didn't know much about the game but as I could kick quite well they played me at back and I was the goal kicker. I was told either to catch the ball and run with it and always pass the ball back; or, catch the ball and kick it into touch. I told them it was crazy! The game started; I was kicking the ball into touch and began enjoying it. After the match, Ossie Williams, one of the Welsh rugby players, suggested that I should go to Cardiff Arms Park and take up the game – even more so when I told him that my mother was Welsh. I said that I would think about it. The CO heard about it and wasn't happy.

The course went well for me and we won the South Wales Cup. The CO played and on the bus going back afterwards he asked me what I wanted to do after demob. 'A professional footballer,' I said. He told me that he knew George Allison, the Arsenal manager at that time, and would give me an introductory letter to him. He also agreed to recommend me for a posting in medical rehabilitation work.

After seven days leave I returned to St. Athans and learned that Squadron Leader Brown had been demobbed. He hadn't written the letter to George Allison but had arranged a posting to Loughborough College. This was the remedial station for the whole of the RAF and had the cream of the PT instructors there.

Loughborough College

I reported to the CO and noticed the name plate on the door, Squadron Leader Dan Maskell. I didn't have a clue who he was at the time but listened to his Wimbledon commentaries for many years later. He welcomed me to the station. I was the first ex-aircrew instructor to be posted to Loughborough. Squadron Leader Brown had given me a good report. There were ten instructors on the station. Patients had only just come out of hospital and would need careful attention for a few weeks. I would have a tutor PTI to iron out any problems.

Loughborough College: from the left Dickie Parfitt, F/Sgt McGowan and F/Sgt Seaton

He took me down to the gym and introduced me to the other PTIs. Among the sporting celebrities were Raich Carter and Peter Doherty who were at that time playing for Derby County. Peter was due for demob; I was to take his place and so he became my tutor. Peter was a very nice chap and very well liked; I had a hard act to follow. Raich on the other hand was a dour man and very rarely did he speak to me; perhaps it was because I was a higher rank. Peter and Raich were demobbed and headed for Wembley to play in the Cup Final.

The patients were all ranks. Each was interviewed by a doctor and I was always present. I was told what could and couldn't be included in their exercises. We had swimming lessons and I suffered the usual fate of a new instructor of being thrown in fully clothed. There were also cycle rides in groups. The PT was enjoyable particularly when I could chivvy some officers!

Chessington
Soon we heard that Loughborough was reverting to its civilian role and it closed as an RAF establishment. We were transferred to No.1 Medical Rehabilitation Unit at Chessington in Surrey. It was next to the zoo. A big advantage of this posting was that I could get home every weekend. Again a few sporting celebrities were on the staff including Bob Davis, Notts Forest and Welsh international and Stan Mercer, Leicester City and England player. We became

*Medical Rehabilitation Unit: chains on legs to strengthen muscles during exercises
(courtesy of Imperial War Museum ref: CH14976)*

good friends. There were women civilian physiotherapists and six doctors including Doc Henderson who was always trying to scrounge flights on 576 Squadron. I became his PTI. I had been promoted to Warrant Officer grade one (WO1) and, as there was a shortage of officers, I was roped in to do some Orderly Officer duties. The Station Warrant Officer told me my duties but I had to tell him that my knowledge of drill and discipline was very limited. 'Hard luck,' he replied; however, one of the instructors, Ted Topping, was a parachute jumping and drill specialist and he showed me the ropes.

I was put in charge of patients of various ranks with polio and fractures of the wrist, fingers, shoulders and elbows. I was introduced to the squad but they couldn't do much because of recent operations. I called out, 'Anybody from Dover?' and up came Phil Peirce whom I still see quite regularly at Royal Air Force Association meetings. He had a damaged shoulder.

Doc Henderson

I was Nigel Henderson's right hand man and we went out together many times. I remember going with him to Kingston upon Thames and in Bentalls, the large department store, he challenged me to a race up the escalators much to the amazement of the customers seeing a flight lieutenant and a WO1 racing upwards. There were a few raised eyebrows. Sometimes he invited me to the Officers' Mess when the CO was absent. There were very few officers and most

No. 1 Medical Rehabilitation Unit Chessington

Relaxing at Chessington

of them were doctors who lived out, except Nigel. One night in walked the CO but as I was the duty Orderly Officer I got away with it.

On one occasion I asked Nigel if he had anything for athlete's foot and he said that he had just the thing. After rummaging around in his surgery he held a small tank in his hand. 'This is something I've invented,' he announced. 'Take off your shoes and socks.' Then he filled the tank with a blue fluid, told me to put my feet in it, plugged a cable into it putting the other end into a socket on the wall. Getting a bit anxious, I said, 'Are you trying to electrocute me?' He laughed and switched it on. By this time I was wishing that I hadn't mentioned my athlete's foot! Apparently this machine operated by passing an electric current through your feet with the power being slowly increased by a rheostat switch. The blue fluid contained iron which was deposited on the inside of your toes and feet which eventually cured the athlete's foot. The only problem was that he forgot to turn the power down low to start and the shock hit me hard! Nigel only laughed.

Life was pretty good at Chessington. Sometimes I took my squad on bicycles to the Thames at Kingston where the RAF had an agreement with a local boat owner; the lads would row and I would supervise them in a motor boat. On Derby Day 1947 we cycled to Epsom racecourse to watch the famous race. On arrival we were given free entry and guided to a good view by the side of the course. We always wore black trousers and white sweaters and were well known in the area; hence the VIP treatment. I remember that 'Airborne' won the Derby that year which was appropriate. In the better weather we were also allowed into Surbiton Swimming Pool. The polio patients were a bit reluctant to swim but I persuaded them with a gentle foot in the rear! The civilians didn't appreciate my 'kindness' but swimming was the best exercise for them. One of my patients was a young Spitfire pilot who was strafing the Germans in Italy when he flew too low and crashed. His brain was shaken up and he had difficulty walking in a straight line.

On one of my weekend passes I contacted Wilf Armory and arranged to play for Folkestone as a guest, hoping that I would become a professional player when demobbed. He was keen and so I played several games for them before demob.

Every Friday afternoon the instructors and doctors would play the patients at volley ball before we all disappeared on a weekend pass. All the patients had to attend. One day I was playing behind Doc Henderson and noticed a patient new to me coughing and going blue in the face before collapsing. I stopped the game. Nigel and I went over to him. The lad couldn't breath so Nigel asked for a safety pin and stuck it through the lad's tongue so that I could hold his tongue out while he was given oxygen, but it was too late. The patient was rushed to hospital but nothing could be done. We all went home a bit subdued.

Demob

Weeks went by, Stan Mercer was demobbed, then Nigel Henderson and then it was my turn. I went to the Demob Centre, collected civilian clothes – a nice double-breasted suit, overcoat, trilby hat, shirts, shoes and underwear – and took

Dickie playing for Folkestone Town in 1946

the train for Dover with 28 days paid demob leave.

One night Ed and I returned home from the pictures. I went to the toilet and passed what I thought was blood. I went to my doctor, Dr. Keottlitz, next day. He examined me, couldn't find anything wrong but took a urine sample. The result several days later showed nothing abnormal so I was sent to hospital for an examination on the Friday. I was playing for Folkestone on the Saturday against Dover which would be a needle match. I had to phone Wilf Armory to tell him I couldn't play; although he had retired, he played in my place but wasn't very happy. Folkestone lost. On the Sunday I had an injection before going into the operating theatre for the examination; however, the operation was put off for some reason and I stayed in bed.

Plastered

Later, the male nurse, who was a Folkestone supporter, came to my bed with two chaps and said, 'This is the bloke you want.' Apparently they were from the artificial limbs department and they wanted somebody from whom they could obtain a good plaster cast of thigh muscles. They were experimenting with new materials for artificial limbs. We went down to their workshop and I stood on a table whilst they put plaster on my thigh. I had to stand there for 15 minutes until it dried then came the tricky part. They had to get the thing off and produced a long knife. To do this they had to go round my leg cutting off the hairs trapped by the plaster which was painful.

My bladder was inspected the next day without anaesthetic which was painful but again nothing wrong was found. Back in bed I asked my male nurse whether beetroot would colour urine. He laughed. I had gone through all that for nothing. As I was still on demob leave I wrote to the Air Ministry and asked for more money as I had spent four days in hospital. I got a letter back saying 'no' but enclosing the King's Badge for members of the armed forces disabled as a result of war service! That was my last contact with the RAF.

POSTSCRIPT

After demob Ed and I settled into married life in the flat over the Co-op butcher's shop in Tower Hamlets.

I began playing at dances again, mainly at Dover Town Hall, with Frank Medhurst and the Crotchets, and for Freddie Overton.

My daughter, Diane, was born on 7 June 1947.

I had played for Folkestone Football Club before the War when I was only 15. In 1947, after my guest appearances, I was signed up by them for 10/- per week! Some people said that I wasn't worth even that. Wilf Armory was the manager and was playing at the time; he was right half and I was left half. At that time Dover had not formed their Kent League Club. Folkestone drew some players from the armed services – some from Shorncliffe Barracks. There was Bill Slater of Wolves and England fame and Jimmy Hill playing in front of me for about a season and a half. Ron Muddle, who was Chairman of Folkestone Football Club, gave me a job as storeman at his works, Folkestone Motor Company. This was to make sure that I was available for football. I played at Folkestone for nearly four years and we won every senior trophy twice.

In 1949 I attended a football coaching course at Birmingham University. Walter Winterbottom, the England team manager, was there with the England team. I joined the Kent Coaching Panel and did some coaching around the county, but not a lot.

Folkestone's Kent Senior Cup Final team, 1949

Stan Wells's mistake

Dover joined the Kent League and was managed by Fred Durrant, a local chap who had played for Queen's Park Rangers. He offered me terms and so I signed. We won the League and Kent Senior Cup. Crowds gave a big welcome to the Senior Cup when it was brought back triumphantly on the club bus. Fred Durrant and I sat on the bonnet of the bus carrying the Cup aloft.

The Dover Express took a photograph at Crabble during a match in October 1952 which showed me and another Dover player, Eric Worthington, who later went to Australia and became their first national football coach before returning to the UK. When the photograph was published in the Express a team mate named Court was named instead of me. Stan Wells, the Editor, was a good friend of mine and so I chastised him for his error. This provoked Stan to write the following letter:-

> *'Dear Mr Parfitt,*
> *It really is a "parfitt" picture even if we did*
> *happen to get "court" out. One really must*
> *wonder, however, how the person could possibly*
> *have failed to score from that position.*
>
> *Yours blindly, Stan Wells.'*

I played for them for three years. In those days Dover drew crowds of 4 or 5,000. Later, I became a director of the old Dover Athletic Football Club, put up with it for about a year, then resigned. There were too many chiefs and not enough indians! Unfortunately, the club became insolvent, which I had forecast, and a new club was formed.

After finishing with football, in 1962 with £100 capital, I started my own business called Gateway Motor Factors in Alexandra Place, Dover. I built the business up over the years, but sold it when I retired at 67.

Despite all that has happened to me in the 55 years since the end of the War, I still remember vividly my small part, and that of my comrades in Bomber Command, in the demise of Adolf Hitler!

Dickie today

ACKNOWLEDGEMENTS

We wish to record our thanks to the Imperial War Museum and the Salvation Army for permission to reproduce photographs and to Merril Lilley for kindly proof reading the text.